Studies in the
Biblical Theology
of Holiness

SANCTIFICATION
AND ITS SYNONYMS

W. T. Purkiser

BEACON HILL PRESS
KANSAS CITY, MISSOURI

Printed in U.S.A.

DEDICATION

To President and Mrs. Roy H. Cantrell
and the faculty and student body of
Bethany Nazarene College,
and to
Dr. and Mrs. Jarrette E. Aycock
through whose generosity many series of Aycock
Lectures have been presented
this little volume is gratefully dedicated

PREFACE

The material in these pages was prepared for delivery as the Aycock Lectures at Bethany Nazarene College during the spring term of 1959. Chapter VI was not one of the original series, but is added to complete the major synonyms for holiness.

Rather extensive footnotes have been supplied for any who might be interested in the f u r t h e r study of the topics discussed. Since the spread of subjects is rather wide, no comprehensive bibliography is included, but bibliographical data is given in the first citation of each work in each chapter.

Scripture quotations not otherwise identified are from the King James Version. However, the American Standard Version, Moffatt, Phillips, the Amplified New Testament, and the Revised Standard Version have been consulted frequently and quoted occasionally. Such quotations are indicated by the standard abbreviation following the reference.

Permission to quote copyrighted materials has been graciously given by the following publishers: The Abingdon Press, quotations from W. E. Sangster, *The Pure in Heart;* and John Bright, *The Kingdom of God;* Beacon Hill Press and the Nazarene Publishing House, quotations from H. E. Brockett, *Scriptural Freedom from Sin;* J. B. Chapman, *The Terminology of Holiness;* A. M. Hills, *Holiness in the Book of Romans;* H. V. Miller, *The Sin Problem;* and H. Orton Wiley, *The Epistle to the Hebrews;* Harper and Brothers, quotations from the Moffatt Translation of the Bible and "Others" from *Masterpieces of Religious Verse;* The Light and Life Press, quotation from G. A. Turner, *The More Excellent Way;* The Macmillan Company, quotation from Vincent Taylor, *Forgiveness and Reconciliation,* and *The New Testament in Modern English,* Phillips; Fleming H. Revell, quotation from R. A. Torrey, *The Person and Work of the Holy Spirit; Theology Today,* editorial quotation from John A. Mackay; the Westminster Press, quotation from H. H. Rowley, *The Unity of the Bible;* Division of Christian Education of the National Council, for quotations from the R.S.V.; and Zondervan Publishing Company for quotations from *The Amplified New Testament.*

The author is deeply indebted to Dr. and Mrs. Jarrette E. Aycock, who provide the semiannual lectureship at Bethany Nazarene College, for the invitation to deliver the lectures; and to Dr. and Mrs. Roy H. Cantrell, and the faculty, staff, and student body of Bethany Nazarene College for their wonderful hospitality and unfailing courtesy during the week of the lectures.

W. T. PURKISER
Nazarene Theological Seminary

CONTENTS

INTRODUCTION

These are exciting times in the Biblical and theological fields. A vast new ferment is making itself felt. There is widespread concern for reconstruction following the collapse of the older religious liberalism.[1] Some of this reconstruction has, to be sure, taken less promising bypaths. But one of the most heartening symptoms of our day is the increased willingness of men to listen to what the writers of Scripture have to say to us. If the movement toward Biblical theology does nothing more than to encourage the systematic study of the meaning of the Word of God, it will have done valiant service for the Church.

These chapters are intended as studies in the Biblical theology of holiness, and particularly of what we may call the synonyms for entire sanctification. The author has the deep conviction that there are two unused sources of strength for the scriptural doctrine of second-blessing holiness. One is the vast network of interconnection between the doctrine of full sanctification and the other vital redemptive themes of the Bible. All of the great teachings of the Word have implications for holiness: God, Christ, the Holy Spirit, the atonement, the resurrection, sin, grace, eschatology, and many others.

The other source of untapped power lies in the fact that the whole Biblical teaching about God's highest purpose for His people is not fully contained in the terms "holy," "holiness," "sanctify," and "sanctification." In the parallel terms and concepts which we have here called synonyms there is a wealth of understanding and insight into the redemptive will of our Heavenly Father. This is recognized in the last two paragraphs of the statement in the "Articles of Faith" of the Church of the Nazarene dealing with entire sanctification:

> Entire sanctification is provided by the b l o o d of Jesus, is wrought instantaneously by faith, preceded by entire consecration; and to this work and state of grace the Holy Spirit bears witness.
>
> This experience is also known by various terms representing its different phases, such as "Christian Perfection," "Perfect Love," "Heart Purity," "The Baptism with the Holy Spirit," "The Fullness of the Blessing," and "Christian Holiness."[2]

CHAPTER I

THE MEANING OF SCRIPTURAL HOLINESS

Before taking up the synonyms for sanctification, we must make a brief study of the main terms, "holy," "holiness," "sanctify," "sanctification." Even the most casual survey of the Bible reveals how central these terms are. In the Old Testament, the root *q-d-sh* and its derivatives are used some 700 times. In the New Testament, the Greek *hagios* and its related terms occur about 400 times.[1] It is clear, then, that no one can profess to understand the teachings of the Scriptures without some grasp of the meaning of these important words.

We note first of all that "holy" is a deeply religious term. It applies most distinctively to God. Careful scholars have shown that holiness is virtually synonymous with divinity, that characteristic or attribute in which God is most essentially God.[2] In fact, this is exactly how Isaiah uses the term when no less than thirty times he speaks of "the Holy One of Israel."[3]

However, we also find hundreds of references to the holiness of things and of people. Here we soon notice a certain two-sidedness in the concept. It relates both to

things and men as belonging to a holy God; and it relates
to persons as they share the character of God or are
"partakers of the divine nature" (II Pet. 1:4). At risk
of a certain degree of oversimplification, we may call
the first use "objective or ceremonial holiness" and the
second use "subjective or ethical sanctification."[4] The
first is consecration; the second is cleansing.

A. CEREMONIAL HOLINESS

There is a sense in which objective or ceremonial
holiness is most characteristic of the Old Testament, and
subjective or ethical holiness is most characteristic of the
New. This distinction must not be carried too far, however. Old Testament scholars have discovered that the
concept of the holy in the Old Testament grew increas-
ingly ethical. This was said many years ago by P. T.
Forsyth:

> The very history of the word holiness in the Old Testa-
> ment displays the gradual transcendence of the idea
> of separation by that of sanctity. It traverses a path
> in which the quantitative idea of *tabu* changes to the
> qualitative idea of active and absolute purity. The reli-
> gious grows ethical, that it may become not only more
> religious but the one religion for the conscience and for
> the world. The one God can only be the holy God.[5]

There are also a number of instances of the ceremonial use of holiness in the New Testament, as by Jesus
in speaking of the Temple (Matt. 24:15) with its gold
and its gifts (Matt. 23:17, 19) as being holy or sanctified. Paul also refers to a believing wife who sanctifies
her unbelieving husband and children (I Cor. 7:14) and
to the sanctification of food (I Tim. 4:5), clear instances
of the objective or ceremonial use of the term. Peter in
the same vein tells his readers to sanctify the Lord their
God in their hearts (I Pet. 3:15).

The frequent description of all believers as *hagion*
or saints, even some who were very carnal (I Cor. 1:2

in relation to I Cor. 3:1-3), shares in this objective or ceremonial use of the term while at the same time it includes an ethical note. There is this strong emphasis, however: the whole thrust of the New Testament is toward the end that those who are saints in name also become saints in nature, that the potential sanctification of all believers become the actual sanctification of the spiritually-minded (I Cor. 2:15; 3:1). From this has arisen the necessary distinction between "initial sanctification" and "entire sanctification" (I Thess. 5:23).

B. Ethical Holiness

It is nevertheless true that the characteristic use of holy and sanctify in the New Testament is subjective and ethical. It includes the whole of the Old Testament meaning, but immeasurably enriches and deepens it. While in the Old Testament the people were frequently told to sanctify themselves (Lev. 11:44, *passim*), or to sanctify the first-born (Exod. 13:2), the altar (Exod. 29:37), the Tabernacle (Lev. 8:10), and the Sabbath day (Deut. 5:12), such use is so rare in the New Testament as to be virtually nonexistent. Instead, sanctification is viewed as an act of God (I Thess. 5:23), wrought by the Holy Spirit (Rom. 15:16, *passim*) through the provision of the atonement in Christ (Heb. 13:12, *passim*). In the New Testament, holiness still involves separation *to God*, setting apart for sacred or divine purposes; but it goes much deeper. It includes separation *from sin*, cleansing or purifying (Eph. 5:25-27).

Since the New Testament is the norm for Christian doctrine, it is well to note that every standard Greek lexicon as well as all leading English dictionaries mention this twofold meaning of sanctification: to set apart or consecrate; and to purify or free from sin.[6] The recognition of this fact led the committee responsible for the Revised Standard Version to restore the term "sanctify"

From his earliest writings to his last brief note to Timothy, Paul insists on the profound subjective and ethical implications of holiness and sanctification. He relates perfection in the quality of trust and abounding love to the establishment of "hearts unblameable in holiness" (I Thess. 3:10-13). Sanctification results in purity of life and freedom from the "lust of concupiscence" (4:3-5), and "uncleanness" and holiness are set in the sharpest possible contrast (4:7-8). At the conclusion of a list of challenging ethical imperatives is the prayer for the entire sanctification of these believers, to result in their blameless preservation, and guaranteed by the faithfulness of God (5:12-24). Sanctification and unrighteousness are seen in the same complete opposition as belief of the truth and strong delusion (II Thess. 2: 11-13).

In the great ethical and doctrinal letters written during his third missionary journey at the high noon of his ministry,[10] Paul makes it even more clear that sanctification involves freedom from the power and presence of sin. Sanctification is joined with wisdom, righteousness, and redemption as implied in the life given us in Christ Jesus (I Cor. 1:30, R.S.V.). Starting with the end result, and following back through the conditions leading to it, Paul writes: "And such were some of you: but ye are washed, but ye are sanctified, but ye are justified in the name of the Lord Jesus, and by the Spirit of our God" (I Cor. 6:11). The analytical approach in this verse leads to a reversal of the usual order of justification and sanctification, which is found, for example, in Romans 1—8; but leaves no doubt as to the connection of sanctification and washing.

Paul gives one of his strong testimonies to personal sanctification in II Cor. 1:12: "For our boast is this, the testimony of our conscience that we have behaved in the world, and still more toward you, with holiness and godly sincerity, not by earthly wisdom but by the grace of God" (RSV).[11] Here we note that holiness is equated with godly sincerity, and concerns behavior and a good conscience in respect both to the world and to the Church. In fact, cleansing from all filthiness of flesh *and spirit* is essential to perfecting holiness (II Cor. 7:1).

Romans 6—8 is Paul's great classic development of the doctrine of sanctification,[12] although the word itself occurs only in 6:19 and 22. Both of these uses disclose the ethical meaning of the term, for in typical Pauline fashion righteousness is contrasted with uncleanness (R.S.V., impurity) and holiness is set over against iniquity (v. 19). Verse 22 speaks for itself: "But now being made free from sin [Greek, *the sin,* i.e., the sin principle], and become servants to God, ye have your fruit unto holiness, and the end everlasting life." Paul explains the ethical portion of Romans (cc. 12—15), not on the basis of any lack of goodness on the part of the Romans, but because it is his special gift in the grace of God so to minister to the gentiles that their offering might be acceptable, "sanctified by the Holy Ghost" (Rom. 15:14-16), still another clear indication that sanctification means freeing from sin.

Ephesians, Philippians, and Colossians are grouped together with Philemon as the Prison Epistles because in all of them Paul mentions his imprisonment; or by themselves they are called the Christological Epistles because of their emphasis on the person and work of Christ. Paul associates the self-giving of Christ in atonement with the sanctifying and cleansing of the Church, washing it and making it holy and without blemish (Eph. 5:25-27). The wider implications of this work of Christ in His Church are developed by the use of a wide range of synonyms for sanctification such as perfection (Eph. 4:12; Phil. 3:12, 15); putting off the old man and putting on the new (Eph. 4:20-24; Col. 3:7-10); and the risen life (Col. 3:1-7).

In I Tim. 2:15, holiness is joined with faith, love, and self-control, all high Christian graces.

The ethical meaning of sanctification is found in Paul's last letter, II Tim. 2:20-21, where those who purge themselves are constituted vessels unto honor, "sanctified, and meet for the master's use, and prepared unto every good work."

In Paul's preaching, as reported in the Book of Acts, there is another example of the ethical use of sanctification. The whole purpose of the apostle's ministry is to turn the gentiles from darkness to light, from the power of Satan to God, so that they might receive forgiveness of sins, "and inheritance among them which are sanctified by faith" in the Lord Jesus Christ (Acts 26:18; cf. also Acts 20:32).

We have, then, clear evidence that Paul continued and expanded the use of sanctification as moral cleansing and freeing from sin which was begun by Jesus in the high priestly prayer.

E. THE GENERAL EPISTLES

In Heb. 2:11, Christ, who sanctifies, and those who are sanctified are said to be all of one Father (*Amplified New Testament*[13]), and Christ is not ashamed to call the sanctified His brethren. In the framework of the Old Testament ceremonial law, the blood of animals which sanctifies "to the purifying of the flesh" is taken as a symbol of the blood of Christ, which alone can "purify your conscience from dead works to serve the living God" (9:13-14, R.S.V.).

The same idea of sanctification as purity is developed in Hebrews 10, where those sanctified by the will of God through the offering of the body of Jesus Christ once for all are perfected forever, and given access into the holiest; and may draw near with true hearts, in "full assurance of faith," with "hearts sprinkled clean from

an evil conscience" and "bodies washed with pure water" (10:10-22, R.S.V.). Set in the context of the ethical
emphasis of chapters 12 and 13 is the call to "follow
peace with all men, and holiness, without which no man
shall see the Lord" (12:14), and the challenge to share
the reproach of Christ, who "suffered outside the gate
in order to sanctify the people through his own blood"
(13:12-13, R.S.V.).

Peter connects the sanctification of the Spirit with
"obedience to Jesus Christ" (I Pet. 1:1-2, R.S.V.), and
sets the Levitical call to holiness firmly in the realm of
the ethical when he says, "But like as he who called you
is holy, [so] be ye yourselves also holy in all manner of
living" (1:15-16, A.R.V.). The practical purpose of redemption is that, having purified our souls by obedience
to the truth through the Spirit, we should love each
other with pure hearts fervently (1:18-23). Being a
chosen generation, a royal priesthood, a holy nation,
God's own people (R.S.V.), we can show forth the
praises (virtues, K.J.V., marg.) of Him who hath called
us out of darkness into his marvelous light (2:9-10).

The very last use of holy in the Bible is in Rev.
22:11, where righteousness is contrasted with evil and
evildoing, and holiness is contrasted with filthiness.

F. The Theological Usage

If, as our study shows, holiness in the New Testament
is most consistently used with an ethical and not a ceremonial meaning, we should expect to find this reflected
in the general Christian tradition. Nor are we disappointed
at this point. Without minimizing in the least the serious
disagreements that exist as to the completeness and mode
of sanctification in this life, we find surprising unanimi-
ty among Protestant theologians to the effect that sanctification is that work of God through His Spirit whereby
the soul of man is freed from the power and presence

of sin. This is clearly shown in the following quotations taken from standard sources, none of which are typically Wesleyan. The arrangement is by date of publication in the editions most readily available:

> Sanctification: the act or process of purifying, cleansing . . . Theologically, sanctification implies spiritual cleansing, moral purification.[14]
>
> In general, sanctification is the work of the Holy Spirit of God, in delivering men from the guilt and power of sin, in consecrating them to the service and love of God, and in imparting to them, initially and progressively, the fruits of Christ's redemption and the graces of a holy life.[15]
>
> By sanctification is ordinarily meant that hallowing of the Christian believer by which he is freed from sin and enabled to realize the will of God in his life.[16]
>
> In technical language sanctification means the operation of the grace by which salvation is conveyed to man, enabling him to be freed and to free himself from sin, and to become like God in heart, will, and thought.[17]
>
> In its wider sense the term *sanctification* includes all those effects of God's Word produced in the heart and life of man, beginning with his rebirth from spiritual death to spiritual life and culminating in spiritual perfection in life eternal.[18]
>
> In Protestant thought, sanctification is the name given to what in Roman theology is called infused grace; but with a difference. In the latter, grace is conceived as a force, sometimes all but impersonal; in the former, sanctification is a continuing activity of God by his personal Spirit. Sanctification is what makes goodness possible; it is not the good and gracious acts of men, but that operation of the Spirit which produces these acts.[19]
>
> Sanctification is thus the perfecting of the Christian life or the progressive cleansing of the soul.[20]

In addition to these quotations from standard reference sources, we shall add the statement of an outstanding Calvinistic theologian, Charles Hodge. Dr. Hodge writes:

> Sanctification in the Westminster Catechism is said to be the work of God's free grace, whereby we are re-

newed in the whole man after the image of God, and are enabled more and more to die unto sin and live unto righteousness.[21]

Dr. Hodge himself says:

Sanctification, therefore, consists in two things: first, the removing more and more the principles of evil still infecting our nature, and destroying their power; and secondly, the growth of the principle of spiritual life until it controls the thoughts, feelings, and acts, and brings the soul into the image of Christ.[22]

Similarly, James S. Stewart, the outstanding New Testament scholar of New College of the Church of Scotland at the University of Edinburgh, states:

Only when union with Christ is kept central is sanctification seen in its true nature, as the unfolding of Christ's own character within the believer's life; and only then can the essential relationship between religion and ethics be understood. In short, the whole meaning of the atonement is here at stake.[23]

A number of these theological definitions of sanctification introduce a progressive element into it, and some imply that it cannot be completed during the course of this earthly life. All, however, agree that the goal of sanctification, as it has been understood in Protestant thought throughout the ages, is the removal of the principle of evil still infecting the nature of the believer, or complete deliverance from sin.

G. A PRESENT POSSESSION

Our discussion thus far does not solve the problem as to the time element involved in our sanctification. At this point we may affirm that there is every Biblical evidence that entire sanctification is as instantaneous and complete in its kind as is justification in its order. Exactly the same type of evidence which points to instantaneous conversion reveals an instantaneous sanctification.[24] What we have mainly been concerned to show

is that the core of the meaning of holiness both in the
Bible and in theology is what has sometimes glibly been
denied: freeing from sin, purity, cleansing.

A quick review of the scripture evidence marshaled
here will reveal something else of great importance. New
Testament sanctification is consistently viewed as occur-
ring within the span of this life, as a part of the total
redemptive scheme of the gospel which relates to the
Church here and now. Zacharias, filled with the Holy
Spirit, summarized the age of the Messiah as providing
the people of God deliverance out of the hands of their
enemies, and the privilege of serving Him "in holiness
and righteousness before him all the days of our life"
(Luke 1: 73-75).[25] The great lesson of the grace of God
that brings salvation to all is that we should "live soberly,
righteously, and godly, in this present world" (Titus
2: 12); and Paul not only testifies that "the law of the
Spirit of life in Christ Jesus hath made me free from the
law of sin and death" (Rom. 8: 2), but calls both God
and the church at Thessalonica to witness "how holy and
righteous and blameless" his behavior had been (I Thess.
2: 10, A.R.V.).

The thing my God doth hate,
    That I no more may do;
Thy creature, Lord, again create,
    And all my soul renew.
My soul shall then, like Thine,
    Abhor the thing unclean,
And, sanctified by love divine,
    Forever cease from sin.

—CHARLES WESLEY

CHAPTER II

THE BAPTISM

WITH THE SPIRIT

In reviewing the teaching of the New Testament on the ethical meaning of sanctification as cleansing or freeing from sin, we noted several clues as to the means or agency whereby the believer is sanctified. God (I Thess. 5:23), the Lord Jesus Christ (Heb. 2:11), the truth (John 17:17), the Blood (Heb. 13:12) are all mentioned as having part in the sanctification of the believer.

Much more frequently, however, it is the Holy Spirit who is identified as the divine Agent in the soul's cleansing (Rom. 15:16; II Thess. 2:13; I Pet. 1:2, *passim*). Sanctification starts with the Spirit, for He is the *Holy* Spirit and the Spirit of holiness (Rom. 1:4). In a word, the baptism and consequent fullness of the Spirit are the means by which entire sanctification is wrought.[1]

A. The Spirit in the Old Testament

As is the case with so many New Testament truths, the study of the Biblical teaching about the Spirit must really begin with the Old Testament. The *ruach* or Spirit of the Lord is present from the second verse of Genesis, bringing order out of chaos, breathing life into man, empowering judges, inspiring prophets, guiding kings, consoling the penitent. Since the great sin of the Old Testament times was polytheism (the worship of many gods), the emphasis of that age was upon the oneness of God (Deut. 6:4). It was Jesus who revealed with utmost clarity the personality of the Holy Spirit in the five great "Paraclete sayings" of the Last Supper discourse.[2] But looking back from this side of Pentecost, we can see how much of the "promise of the Father" (Acts 1:4) was recorded in the prophets, and how carefully the Old Testament writings safeguard the doctrine of the Spirit.

While it is true that in the earlier pages of the Old Testament the Spirit of God would come upon and use men of inferior moral quality (Samson and Saul, for example), in the later pages there is a growing recognition of the spiritual uplift brought by the Spirit. Indeed, the New Testament title "Holy Spirit" is actually used in the Old Testament three times (Ps. 51:11; Isa. 63: 10, 11). The Spirit is to be poured out from on high, and the wilderness will become a fruitful field, with justice, righteousness, peace, quietness, and trust (Isa. 32:15-17). He will come upon the descendants of Israel like water on thirsty land and streams in the desert (Isa. 44:3). In fact, God's covenant with Israel, in its essence, is that His Spirit will continually be with His people (Isa. 59:21).

As the prophetic movement deepened, the vision of the Spirit grew. Ezekiel's great message of hope spoke of a day when Israel would be cleansed from all her uncleanness and idols by God's Spirit within, providing power to walk in His statutes and to keep His ordinances (36:25-29). God's promise is that He will no longer hide His face from His people, but will pour out His Spirit upon them (39:29).

In Zech. 12:10, we read that the pouring out of God's Spirit upon the house of David and the inhabitants of Jerusalem, "the spirit of grace and of supplications," will cause tears of repentance to flow from those who pierced the Lord of glory.

The great eschatological sign that the end time has dawned, says the prophet Joel, will be the pouring out of the Spirit of God upon all flesh without distinction as to race or vocation (Joel 2:28-32).

B. CHRIST AND THE SPIRIT

As the predicted day drew near, the work of the Spirit received greater prominence. In all His manhood our Saviour was dependent upon the Spirit: conceived of the Spirit in the Virgin Mary (Matt. 1:18; Luke 1:35); anointed by the Spirit at His baptism (Mark 1:10, *passim*); led by the Spirit into the wilderness of temptation (Luke 4:1); identified in all four Gospels as the One who baptizes with the Holy Spirit (Matt. 3:11; Mark 1:8; Luke 3:16; John 1:33); His teaching and work such that it might all be described as being always "in the power of the Spirit" (Luke 4:14).

Jesus himself spoke of the Holy Spirit only five times before the Last Supper discourse recorded in John 13—16.[3] On that great occasion, the Lord promised the Comforter or Advocate[4] to those who love Him and keep His commandments, for the world cannot receive Him (14:14-17). He is the Spirit of truth, and will bring all things to remembrance which Jesus spoke (14:26). He will bear witness to Christ (15:26-27), and lead into all truth (16:13-15). In respect to the world, He will convict of sin, of righteousness, and of judgment (16:7-11). In all, as Archibald Hunter has remarked, the Spirit comes not so much to supply Jesus' absence as to accomplish His presence (14:21-23),[5] inasmuch as the fullness of the Spirit is the fullness of God and the realized presence of the indwelling Christ (John 14: 23 and Eph. 3: 16-19).

C. CHRIST'S BAPTISM

That the baptism with the Holy Spirit is in a special way the baptism of Christ is a certain note in the New Testament. We hear it first from the lips of John the Baptist: "I indeed baptize you with water unto repentance: but he that cometh after me is mightier than I, whose shoes I am not worthy to bear: he shall baptize you with the Holy Ghost, and with fire: whose fan is in his hand, and he will throughly purge his floor" (Matt. 3: 11-12; cf. also Mark 1: 8; Luke 3: 16-17; John 1: 33).

We hear it again in our Lord's own words: "And being assembled together with them, commanded them that they should not depart from Jerusalem, but wait for the promise of the Father, which, saith he, ye have heard of me. For John truly baptized with water; but ye shall be baptized with the Holy Ghost not many days hence" (Acts 1: 4-5).

We listen to it once more from the lips of Peter, as he reports to the Jerusalem church on the events at the house of Cornelius in Caesarea: "Then remembered I the word of the Lord, how that he said, John indeed baptized with water; but ye shall be baptized with the Holy Ghost" (Acts 11: 16). The actual effusion of the Spirit at Pentecost is also explained by Peter as the work of the exalted Christ: "Therefore being by the right hand of God exalted, and having received of the Father the promise of the Holy Ghost, he hath shed forth this, which ye now see and hear" (Acts 2: 33).[6]

The importance of the two baptisms, of John and of Jesus, must not be overlooked. There are both comparison and contrast to be found here. "To baptize" means variously "to dip, to wash, to cleanse, to purify." A baptism with the Holy Spirit as with fire could no more be a gradual, never-completed process than could a baptism with water. Both, in the very nature of the case, must be acts which take place at a given time.

The contrasts are perhaps even greater, and are symbolized by the elements involved, water and fire. The baptism of John is a baptism of repentance for the remission of sins (Mark 1:4). The baptism of Jesus is a baptism with the Holy Spirit for the purging of the "floor," as fire throughout Scripture is symbolic of cleansing from deep dross. It is almost axiomatic that the two baptisms could not occur together, and in the chronology of the soul as well as the chronology of history, the baptism of repentance for the remission of sins must precede the baptism with the Spirit for the purifying of the heart (cf. Acts 15:8-9).

In Acts 2:4, the baptism with the Holy Spirit is further defined as being "filled with the Holy Ghost." In fact, the description of Pentecost in the Book of Acts is not "baptized with" but "filled with" the Spirit.[7] True, there is a difference in these phrases which must be remembered. "Filled with the Spirit" describes not only an act in which that fullness is first accomplished; it also describes the state or condition which results from the initial filling. As Thomas Cook points out:

> 'Baptized with' and 'filled with the Holy Ghost' are often convertible terms in the Acts of the Apostles, but it is instructive to note that they are not always so. The apostles received but one baptism but they were 'filled' with the Spirit over and over again. The baptism of the Holy Ghost was, and still is, a sort of initiatory rite to the life of Pentecostal service, and fullness and victory. Christian life begins at Calvary, but effective service begins at Pentecost.[8]

In the record of the fulfillment of the promise of the Father in Acts 2, we should not forget that there are two aspects to Pentecost as there described. There is, first, what might be called the historical aspect. Pentecost was the beginning of a new era, the inauguration of a new dispensation, the birthday of the Christian Church. As such it was unique and unrepeatable, just as the giving of the law at Sinai. And as such, it was accompanied with remarkable dispensational signs—the noise of the rushing mighty wind, the cloven tongues as of fire, the capacity to speak languages which had not been learned—just as there were the cloud of smoke and the roll of thunder and the flash of lightning at Sinai.

The second aspect of Pentecost is what might be called the existential aspect. This is what Pentecost accomplished in the hearts and lives of the individual members of the 120 there gathered. In the existential meaning of Pentecost, the dispensational signs become symbols of what happens in experience: the wind symbolizes the power of the Spirit, the fire testifies to the purity He brings, and the tongues typify the gifts for service which He gives (I Cor. 12:4-11).

In connection with the gift of other languages, it should be noted that there are no "unknown" tongues here. In fact, the languages are listed in which the crowd heard "the wonderful works of God" (Acts 2:7-11). So far from there being unknown tongues involved, the gift was actually given to prevent unknown tongues. For if the Galilean disciples had preached in their north-Palestinian dialect to that cosmopolitan crowd, they would have been speaking a tongue unknown to most of the company. The Spirit gave this gift so that there would be no "unknown tongues" spoken at Pentecost.

D. Paul and the Nature of the Spirit's Work

It is in the writings of Paul that we find the most complete description of the place of the Holy Spirit in the life of the Christian. It has been said that one might as well try to describe modern civilization without electricity as the Christianity of St. Paul apart from the Spirit of God.[9]

In understanding Paul aright, and indeed the whole of the New Testament doctrine of the Spirit, we must keep two extremes in balance. One is the continuity of the Spirit's work in all Christian experience, as indicated, for example, in Rom. 8:9, "Now if any man have not the Spirit of Christ, he is none of his."

The other point of reference is the fact that the fullness of the Spirit produces effects in the believer's experience which are not just quantitatively but qualitatively different from the new birth: "For the law of the Spirit of life in Christ Jesus has set me free from the law of sin and death. For God has done what the law, weakened by the flesh, could not do: sending his own Son in the likeness of sinful flesh and for sin, he condemned [literally, 'doomed'] sin in the flesh" (Rom. 8:2-3, R.S.V).

Let us look first at the continuity of the Spirit's ministry. Every phase of the Christian life is the work of the Holy Spirit. He convicts of sin (John 16:8). He reveals the Saviour through the Word (I Cor. 2:10-13). He inspires faith (John 15:26). He regenerates and renews the repentant, believing heart (John 3:6-7; Titus 3:5). He witnesses to the adoption of the believer as a child of God (Rom. 8:15-16). He leads the children of God (Rom. 8:14). He brings the believer to a place of full consecration (Rom. 12:1-2). He inspires the hunger and thirst after righteousness which leads to prayer for full cleansing (Matt. 5:6; Ps. 51:10-11). He sanctifies entirely (Rom. 15:16). He helps us with our infirmities and makes intercession with groanings which cannot be uttered (Rom. 8:26-27). From the earliest dawn of religious consciousness down to the last glorious moment on earth when He transforms our earthly bodies into the image of our resurrected Lord (Rom. 8:11), there is a continuity in the Spirit's redemptive work (cf. Phil. 1:6). Even before Pentecost, Jesus said to His disciples concerning the Spirit of truth: "But ye know him; for he dwelleth with you, and shall be in you" (John 14:17). We are born of the Spirit no less than baptized with the Spirit.

At the other end of the scale is the equally important truth that the fullness of the Spirit is not merely more of the same thing we have in the new birth. There is a qualitative difference between being born of the Spirit and baptized with the Spirit.

In the birth of the Spirit there is the impartation of a new life. "Blessed be the God and Father of our Lord Jesus Christ, which according to his abundant mercy hath begotten us again unto a lively hope by the resurrection of Jesus Christ from the dead" (I Pet. 1:3). In the baptism with the Spirit there is the destruction of an old nature. "And God, which knoweth the hearts, bare them witness, giving them the Holy Ghost, even as he did unto us; and put no difference between us and them, purifying their hearts by faith" (Acts 15:8-9). As the inimitable Uncle Bud Robinson—the "Will Rogers of the holiness movement"—used to put it: "When I was converted, I got something I'd never had; when I was sanctified wholly, I lost something I'd always had."

E. Birth of the Spirit and Baptism with the Spirit

The important distinction between the birth of the Spirit and the baptism with the Spirit has been recognized clearly outside the holiness churches. Thus, Bishop H. C. G. Moule, the devout and scholarly prelate of the Church of England, wrote:

> We gather very plainly that "the Filling" is not identical in idea, whether or no it coincides in time, with the initial work of the Spirit as the Life-Giver. The Filling is always seen as taking place where there is already present the New Birth; and the possession of that Birth is thus the occasion for a holy desire and longing to possess in some sense the Filling.[10]

Again, the Bishop says:

The believer, already a believer by the Spirit's lifegiving operation, is now also "sealed" as the property of his Master by the same Spirit's developed possession of him. And this possession, with its holy fruit, is the "earnest" of his full possession of his God for ever in eternity; the "first-fruits" of the harvest of "life everlasting" which is to be reaped "of the Spirit" then at length.[11]

The same point of distinction between the birth of the Spirit and the baptism with the Spirit is noted by Reuben A. Torrey, the first president of the Moody Bible Institute in Chicago, in his volume *The Person and Work of the Holy Spirit:*

It is evident that the baptism with the Holy Spirit is an operation of the Holy Spirit distinct and additional to His regenerating work. . . . A man may be regenerated by the Holy Spirit and still not be baptized with the Holy Spirit. In regeneration, there is the impartation of life by the Spirit's power, and the one who receives it is saved: in the baptism with the Holy Spirit, there is the impartation of power, and the one who receives it is fitted for service.[12]

F. Purity Through the Spirit

There is obviously a missing note in Dr. Torrey's statement, for the Spirit cleanses those whom He empowers. But it is important to note that by nature and function birth and baptism are distinctively different operations of the Spirit of God. The baptism or being filled with the Spirit is not simply more of the same which was received at conversion. Fullness by definition implies exclusion, the expulsion of all foreign elements. A friend of mine went to Palestine some years ago, and brought home a bottle filled with water from the Jordan River. Before that bottle could be filled with the Jordan, everything other than water had to be expelled, and was in fact expelled in the very act of filling the container. It is true, not all of the Jordan was in the bottle—but all that was in the bottle was the Jordan.

In a similar way, the divine Spirit cleanses the heart He fills by expelling all sin, native as well as acquired, and by His own abiding presence keeps it clean. It is almost inconceivable that the spirit of man can be thoroughly conditioned by the Spirit of God and at the same time stained and tinctured by carnal pride and ambition, selfish anger, envy, resentment, animosity, bitterness, inner conflict, lovelessness, and all the other evil brood of the carnal mind. As Vincent Taylor has said, "The broad stream of New Testament teachings concerning men 'filled with the Spirit' is related to conduct, duties, service, insight, and saintliness. The Spirit is 'Holy,' and His power is directed to the sanctification and enrightment of life."[13]

G. THE POWER OF THE SPIRIT

However, the power of the Spirit must not be overlooked. The word for *Spirit,* in both Old and New Testaments, also means *wind,* alike in its life-giving sense of "breath" and in its suggestion of power. In the Old Testament the human weakness of the flesh is contrasted with the divine power of the Spirit (Isa. 31:3). In the New Testament, the Spirit is like the wind, which blows where it wills (John 3:8), and one of the dispensational signs of Pentecost was the sound of a "rushing mighty wind" (Acts 2:2). We who live in tornado country, as those who live in areas exposed to hurricanes, can testify to the power of a rushing mighty wind. The Holy Spirit is the Spirit of power, of love, and of a sound mind (II Tim. 1:7).

It is a point to ponder that our Lord in each of His references to the soon-coming baptism with the Spirit made the outreach in power of a sanctified life the prime motivating factor. When the Spirit comes, His distinctive ministry includes convicting the world of sin, of righteousness, and of judgment (John 16:8-11). Jesus sends "the promise of the Father," and states as its accompaniment that His disciples will be "clothed with power from on high" (Luke 24:49, R.S.V.). It is the power of the Holy Spirit coming upon the apostles which makes them witnesses to Christ, in Jerusalem, and in all Judea, and in Samaria, and unto the uttermost parts of the earth (Acts 1:8). President John A. Mackay of Princeton Seminary has said:

> A Christian filled with the Holy Ghost is the redemptive counterpart of the fanatical devotee of political religion. People consumed by the inner fire of the Spirit are the counterpart in human life of the smashed atom which releases cosmic force . . . What we need, in a word, within the Christian Church, if the Church is to match this hour, is Christians who are utterly Christian, in whom the full potentiality of spiritual life becomes manifest. Only thus will the Christian men and women of today be linked to the saints of yesterday.[14]

H. RECEIVING THE SPIRIT

One of the most instructive passages in the Book of Acts is the account of Paul's return to the city of Ephesus, after having visited it briefly on his way from Corinth to the Passover in Jerusalem, and after leaving there his close companions and fellow laborers, Aquila and Priscilla. Finding a group of disciples, about twelve in all, Paul addressed them a most searching question: "Have ye received the Holy Ghost since ye believed?" (Acts 19:2)

This question is translated in the revised versions, "Did you receive the Holy Spirit when you believed?" It must be admitted that the Greek will bear either rendering, although Charles Ewing Brown has argued strongly and cogently for the former in an appendix to *The Meaning of Sanctification*.[15] Essentially, however, two facts remain crystal-clear whichever translation be preferred: these men were believers, and their faith is acknowledged by the Apostle Paul; and they had not received the Holy Spirit in the sense in which Paul intended.

It is not uncommon to find doubt expressed as to the actual conversion of these Ephesians. A careful reading of the passage, on the contrary, makes it crystal-clear that these disciples were indeed believers in a true sense. As F. F. Bruce notes concerning the term disciple: "This word standing alone meant not 'disciples of John' but 'disciples of Jesus,' whatever the defects in their knowledge might be."[16] "The disciples were called Christians first in Antioch" (Acts 11:26).

Nor can the fact that the Ephesian disciples had been baptized only with John's baptism be urged against the genuineness of their Christian faith, for Apollos, who labored in Ephesus prior to this time, is described as a man "instructed in the way of the Lord; and being fervent in the spirit, he spake and taught diligently the things of the Lord, knowing only the baptism of John" (Acts 18:25).

True, the men were woefully ignorant about the Holy Spirit, as ignorant as Dwight L. Moody said he was for years after his conversion.[17] As Mr. Moody further said:

> I venture to say that there are very many, who, if you were to ask them, "Have you received the Holy Ghost since you believed?" would reply, "I don't know what you mean by that." They would be like the twelve men down at Ephesus, who had never understood the peculiar relation of the Spirit to the sons of God in this dispensation.[18]

One further fact concerning the prior conversion of the Ephesians must be noted. That is the rebaptism of the group by Paul, *before* the Holy Spirit came upon them. If the coming of the Spirit was, as has been alleged, only their regeneration, then St. Paul baptized a group of unconverted people in the name of the Lord

Jesus Christ. That this has been done since is not to be denied, but that Paul started the custom is incredible.

Not only is the fact of the conversion of the Ephesians indicated in Paul's question; there is the further fact that there is a "receiving" of the Holy Spirit which does not occur at the time of the new birth. Jesus said concerning the Comforter: "Whom the world cannot receive, because it seeth him not, neither knoweth him," while, on the contrary, the pre-Pentecostal disciples had an experience in which "he dwelleth with you, and shall be in you" (John 14:17).

It is instructive to note that the New Testament speaks no less than twelve times of believers "receiving" the Holy Spirit, and in almost every instance with evidence of a prior conversion on the part of those who were to receive Him. There is in the Greek term (*lambano*) itself a sense of welcoming, of taking by one's own desire. The heavenly Comforter comes not as an unwelcome intruder, but only as an invited Guest, to make His home with and within.

In this chapter, then, we have learned of the great importance of the doctrine of the Holy Spirit in the New Testament, and of the fact that the baptism or fullness of the Spirit means not only power but purity. It is, moreover, an experience only a Christian can receive. Without it, the believer's life is limited and stunted. Only in the fullness of the Spirit is there the maximum development of spiritual stature and grace.

> *Oh, come, and dwell in me,*
>   *Spirit of power within!*
> *And bring the glorious liberty*
>   *From sorrow, fear, and sin.*
> *The seed of sin's disease,*
>   *Spirit of health, remove,*
> *Spirit of finished holiness,*
>   *Spirit of perfect love.*
>
> —CHARLES WESLEY

CHAPTER III

PURITY
OF HEART

The fullness of the Spirit, as we have said, implies not only power but purity. The Spirit cleanses as He communicates His power in himself. This is also the characteristic New Testament meaning of holiness. It leads us to our next synonym for sanctification: purity of heart, or heart cleansing.

It is to be noted that the Bible uses the terms clean, pure, cleanse, and purify in a ceremonial sense at times, to indicate that which is free from defilement or impurity of the sort forbidden in the law of Moses. Thus there are clean and unclean animals mentioned in the Old Testament (Lev. 11:1-30). After their recovery, lepers were required to be cleansed by the priests, for leprosy brought ceremonial defilement (Lev. 14:1-32). A Jew who touched blood, or a dead body, or who walked over a grave was unclean.

When Paul made his last visit to Jerusalem, he was requested to take four men who had made vows, and to purify himself with them in order that the Jewish Christians might see that the apostle to the gentiles himself kept the ceremonial law and did not teach men to forsake it (Acts 21:23-26; cf. I Cor. 9:20).

We are apt to view the ceremonial law of the Old Testament with wonder, forgetting that in the infancy of the race God had to teach by object lessons. The effect of centuries of concern for ceremonial cleanness was to root deeply the great truth that there is a difference, vitally important, between the sacred and the secular, the spiritual and the profane.

A. MORAL PURITY IN THE OLD TESTAMENT

Of far greater concern to us are the many times the Bible uses these great words in an obviously ethical sense, to mean pure and clean in respect to the moral and spiritual defilement of sin and unrighteousness. Four verses from the Old Testament clearly indicate this important meaning, three from the Psalms and one from Ezekiel. Psalms 24, attributed to David by its Hebrew title, describes the true citizens of God's spiritual kingdom, of whom the question is asked: "Who shall ascend into the hill of the Lord? or who shall stand in his holy place?" The answer is, "He that hath clean hands, and a pure heart; who hath not lifted up his soul unto vanity, nor sworn deceitfully" (vv. 3-4). Of note here is the mention first of clean hands, and then of a pure heart. Hands symbolize the deeds of the outer life; the heart, which is to be pure (*bar*), refers to the inner nature.

David's great prayer of penitence in Psalms 51 offers the next instance of the mention of a clean heart in the Old Testament. Wrung from the Psalmist's soul by the tragedy of his sin with Bath-sheba, the psalm begins with a prayer for forgiveness, and the blotting out of his transgressions.

But dealing with the symptoms will not cure the disease. Therefore the prayer deepens into a petition for a radical cleansing: "Purge me with hyssop [the shrub used to sprinkle the blood from the sacrificial altar], and I shall be clean: wash me, and I shall be whiter than snow. Create in me a clean heart, O God; and renew a right spirit within me" (vv. 7, 10). The Hebrew term for clean in these references, *taher,* is defined in the Harkavy *Hebrew and Chaldee Dictionary to the Old Testament* as "to be clean . . . in a moral sense: to be pure, sinless . . . to make clean, to cleanse . . . to purify."[1]

Psalms 73 is credited to Asaph, David's great musician. It is classified as one of the "Wisdom Psalms," for it deals with the great problem posed by the prosperity of the wicked and the adversity of the righteous. However, the first verse expresses the Psalmist's faith, and by anticipation the conclusion to which he comes: "Truly God is good to Israel, even to such as are of a clean heart."

Some years ago William E. Sangster made a study of John Wesley's doctrine of entire sanctification for a Ph.D. degree at the University of London. Some of the conclusions he reached have been challenged by other equally competent Wesley scholars. However, in the course of this study Dr. Sangster compiled a list of thirty Biblical texts upon which Mr. Wesley placed major reliance in proving his position.[2]

Only one of these texts is found in the Old Testament. "Then will I sprinkle clean water upon you, and ye shall be clean: from all your filthiness, and from all your idols, will I cleanse you. A new heart also will I give you, and a new spirit will I put within you: and I will take away the stony heart out of your flesh, and I will give you an heart of flesh. And I will put my spirit within you, and cause you to walk in my statutes, and ye shall keep my judgments, and do them" (Ezek. 36: 25-27).

In the *Plain Account of Christian Perfection,* Wesley included a hymn by his brother Charles based upon this Old Testament promise:

The sanctifying Spirit pour,
    To quench my thirst, and wash me clean;
Now, Saviour, let the gracious shower
    Descend, and make me pure from sin.

Purge me from every sinful blot:
    My idols all be cast aside:
Cleanse me from every evil thought,
    From all the filth of self and pride.

The hatred of the carnal mind
    Out of my flesh at once remove:
Give me a tender heart, resigned,
    And pure, and full of faith and love.[3]

B. PURITY IN THE NEW TESTAMENT

It is, of course, in the New Testament that the vision of a pure heart reached its fulfillment. The Greek has two words which express the idea of purity or cleansing. Each of these, as in the Old Testament, may mean merely ceremonial cleanness; but usually they describe moral and spiritual purity.

One of these Greek terms, less frequently used than the other, is *hagnos* and its derivative forms. It comes from the same root as *hagios*, the term for holy which we surveyed in Chapter I. However, *hagnos* stands for purity only, and not for the double idea of consecration and cleansing as implied in *hagios* and its related terms.

W. E. Vine defines *hagnos* as "pure, free from defilement, not contaminated."[4] This is the term James uses when he refers back to Ps. 24:4: "Draw nigh to God, and he will draw nigh to you. Cleanse your hands, ye sinners; and purify [*hagnisate*] your hearts, ye double minded" (Jas. 4:8). Peter uses the same term: "Seeing ye have purified [*hegnikotes*] your souls in obeying the truth through the Spirit unto unfeigned love of the brethren, see that ye love one another with a pure [*katharas*] heart fervently" (I Pet. 1:22). John likewise states concerning the Christian's blessed hope of seeing Christ as He is and being like Him: "And every man that hath this hope in him purifieth [*hagnizei*] himself, even as he is pure [*hagnos*]" (I John 3:3). It is worthy of notice that in these three verses we have three objects of purification or cleansing: the heart (*kardia*), the soul (*psychas*), and the self (*heauton*).

The major New Testament term for cleansing or purification is *katharizo, katharos,* and derivatives. Hermann Cremer, who treats this term exhaustively, defines it as meaning "pure, clean, without stain, without spot."[5] It is used in its ethical sense in each of the major divisions of the New Testament: in the Gospels and Acts, the Pauline Epistles, and the General Epistles and Revelation.[6]

Katharos was the term Jesus used in the sixth beatitude: "Blessed are the pure in heart: for they shall see God" (Matt. 5:8). Since all other beatitudes refer to actual classes or groups of people in this life, it is hard to see why the pure in heart should be made an exception, as some have done, and relegated to the heavenly state.

In our study of the baptism with the Spirit, we had occasion to note Peter's testimony to the coming of the Spirit upon Cornelius and his household in what New Testament scholars know as "the gentile Pentecost."

We may recognize something of a transitional character in the experience of Cornelius, overlapping as it does the two dispensations of the Son and of the Spirit. However when we add together all Luke says about Cornelius in the three accounts he gives (Acts 10, 11, and 15), we get an overwhelming sense of the force of this testimony to the spiritual nature of a gentile army officer. He was a devout man, who feared God and prayed constantly (10:2). His prayers were heard in heaven (10:4). He was not to be called common nor unclean (10:15). He feared God, worked righteousness, and was accepted with Him (10:35). He knew the word of the gospel (10:36). The gift of the Spirit was a witness to him and to his household that they had believed, borne by God, who knows the hearts (15:8). The use of "shall be saved" (15:11) is in regard to final salvation, as Peter says "we [also] shall be saved," and Paul says, "God hath . . . chosen us to salvation through sanctification of the Spirit and belief of the truth" (II Thess. 2:13).

Upon men and women of this character, the Holy Spirit came in a manner comparable to Pentecost. Peter described it for the church in Jerusalem: "And God, which knoweth the hearts, bare them witness, giving them the Holy Ghost, even as he did unto us; and put no difference between us and them, purifying their hearts by faith" (Acts 15:8-9). The term Peter used for purifying was *katharisas*. In Dr. Richard Taylor's memorable words, "Peter went right to the heart of Pentecost by showing that Pentecost goes right to the heart."[7] This it does in the completeness of its cleansing from all inner sin.

C. PAUL'S USE OF "KATHARAS"

As we turn to Paul's writings, we find a number of significant uses of cleansing and purifying in relation to the inner self. In II Cor. 7:1 we read: "Having therefore these promises, dearly beloved, let us cleanse ourselves from all filthiness of the f l e s h and spirit, perfecting holiness in the fear of God."

Here, as noted in Chapter I, cleansing from all filthiness is related to perfecting holiness. That we are urged to cleanse *ourselves* ought to lead to no doctrine of sanctification by works, any more than the exhortation, "Save yourselves from this untoward generation," (Acts 2:40) should lead to a doctrine of salvation by works. In each case the thought is that of taking advantage of the means God has provided for salvation and cleansing.

In Eph. 5:25-27 there is another correlation of sanctification and cleansing: "Husbands, love your wives, even as Christ also loved the church, and gave himself for it; that he might sanctify and cleanse it with the washing of water by the word, that he might present it to himself a glorious church, not having spot, or wrinkle, or any such thing; but that it should be holy and without blemish."

In the Pastoral Epistles we find an interesting cluster of references in which pure, purify, clean, and cleanse are used. The purpose and end of the commandment is love out of a pure heart, together with a good conscience and genuine faith (I Tim. 1:5). Deacons are to hold the revelation of the faith in a pure or clean conscience (I Tim. 3:9), a phrase which Paul uses of himself, serving God with a pure conscience (II Tim. 1:3). The young Timothy is counseled to turn his back on "the turbulent desires of youth" (Phillips), and follow righteousness, faith, love, and peace with those who "call on the Lord out of a pure heart" (II Tim. 2:22).

To Titus, Paul writes that to the pure all things are pure (1:15), and reminds him that the grace of God has appeared to all men, bringing salvation, and teaching them to live in soberness, righteousness, and godliness while renouncing all worldly lusts. Affirming the deity of Christ—"awaiting our blessed hope, the appearing of the glory of our great God and Savior Jesus Christ"—Paul summarizes the redemptive purpose of our Lord as being "to redeem us from all iniquity and to purify for himself a people of his own who are zealous for good deeds" (2:11-14, R.S.V.).

D. JOHN AND CLEANSING FROM ALL SIN

In I John 1: 7 and 9 we find the last two uses of the term we shall have time to examine: "But if we walk in the light, as he is in the light, we have fellowship one with another, and the blood of Jesus Christ his Son cleanseth us from all sin. If we confess our sins, he is faithful and just to forgive us our sins, and to cleanse us from all unrighteousness." Since these verses come from a passage often quoted in defense of the thesis that there is no freedom from sin and sinning in this life, it must have a closer study than we have given other references.

I John 1: 8 and 10 are often lifted from their context and quoted to "prove" that there is no deliverance from sin in this world: "If we say that we have no sin, we deceive ourselves, and the truth is not in us. If we say that we have not sinned, we make him a liar, and his word is not in us." Standing alone, these words would appear fatal to any truly Wesleyan interpretation of the Christian life.

It should go without saying that it is extremely dangerous to lift verses from their contexts and set them up as "proof" texts. In the actual discussion of Scripture, it is of course necessary to quote typical or representative verses, for to read or quote the total context would be too time-consuming. However, the context must be kept in mind in the citation of any Biblical passage, and no verse quoted to support views which are out of harmony with the context of the verse itself. This is exactly what happens when verses 8 and 10 are lifted from their setting and treated alone.

In studying I John 1: 7-10, we should first observe that this passage is deductive and analytical, not inductive and synthetic. That is, it does not start with man in sin and trace the path from sin to holiness. It rather starts with God in the blazing light of His perfect holiness, and surveys the steps whereby the sinner has bee'

brought to fellowship with God. Because the passage is
God-centered rather than man-centered, the order of
topics is opposite to the order in which we usually ar-
range them.

John starts with an established fellowship with God
in light and holiness, a fellowship wherein there is a constant walk and a continual cleansing from all sin (v. 7).
But from what sin are we cleansed and kept clean? If
we say we have no sin from which we need to be cleansed,
as is sometimes claimed even today,[8] "we deceive ourselves, and the truth is not in us" (v. 8). But before God
deals with the problem of inner sin (the sin which "we
have," as contrasted with the sins which we do), the
problem of committed sins must be met. Hence, "if we
confess our sins, he is faithful and just to forgive us our
sins, and to cleanse us from all unrighteousness" (v. 9).
That we needed this forgiveness is testified to by both
John and Paul: "If we say we have not sinned, we may
make him a liar, and his word is not in us" (v. 10); "For
all have sinned, and come short of the glory of God"
(Rom. 3:23). It should be noted that these last two
verses do not say, "If we say we are not sinning (daily,
in word, thought, and deed)," and, "For all are sinning."
They both have reference to a past state, normally ended
at regeneration.

Should we now desire to read the passage from the
human point of view rather than from the divine side,
we should begin with the human predicament: "If we
say that we have not sinned, we make him a liar, and his
word is not in us" (v. 10). "If we confess our sins, he
is faithful and just to forgive us our sins, and to cleanse
us from all unrighteousness" (v. 9). "If we say that we
have no sin, we deceive ourselves, and the truth is not
in us" (v. 8). "But if we walk in the light, as he is in
the light, we have fellowship one with another, and the
blood of Jesus Christ his Son cleanseth us from all sin"
(v. 7).

E. THE HEART AS THE OBJECT OF CLEANSING

Before concluding, it is necessary to examine what in man is the object of this divine cleansing. Self, soul, and conscience are all mentioned. Most frequently, however, the heart is indicated.

The heart is easily one of the most important, and at the same time one of the most misunderstood, of the Biblical terms relating to man. In popular thought it is confined almost entirely to the feelings or emotions. In the Bible, however, it is the comprehensive term employed to describe the real human person in all aspects of his inner life. "Where we say 'person' the Bible says 'heart,' and by that it means the personal totality in its essential relation to God and to the neighbour."[9]

As Robert B. Girdlestone summarizes: "The heart, according to Scripture, not only includes the motives, feelings, affections, and desires, but also the will, the aims, the principles, the thoughts, and the intellect of man. In fact, it embraces the whole inner man."[10]

Concerning the use of heart for the self, C. Ryder Smith states: "This means that 'heart' comes the nearest of the New Testament terms to mean 'person,' but also, as usual in Bible psychology, that 'will' takes precedence over intellect and emotion. *Kardia* (heart) can be used to mean 'the inward man' considered as a whole."[11]

A few Biblical examples will make this breadth of meaning quite apparent:

"The fool hath said in his heart, There is no God" (Ps. 14:1).

"So that thou incline thine ear unto wisdom, and apply thine heart to understanding" (Prov. 2:2).

"As he thinketh in his heart, so is he" (Prov. 23:7).

"The heart is deceitful above all things, and desperately wicked: who can know it?" (Jer. 17:9)

"All men mused in their hearts of John, whether he were the Christ, or not" (Luke 3:15).

"And they said one to another, Did not our heart burn within us, while he talked with us by the way, and while he opened to us the scriptures?" (Luke 24:32)

"Let not your heart be troubled, neither let it be afraid" (John 14:27).

"But God be thanked, that ye were the servants of sin, but ye have obeyed from the heart that form of doctrine which was delivered you" (Rom. 6:17).

Here, and in a multitude of other references which might be given, the heart thinks, ponders, chooses, feels, and obeys. Intellect, will, sensibilities are all involved in the heart. The total self, judging, purposing, feeling, experiencing, is what is cleansed and made pure through Christ and His perfect atonement. The heart is represented throughout Scripture in three conditions: it may be deceitful and desperately wicked, the natural heart; it may be divided, "double minded," the regenerate but unsanctified heart; or it may be pure, the sanctified heart.

The goal of all redemption is to make possible the experience of a pure heart. In the Christian religion, anything *less* than this is *subnormal*. Anything *other* than this is *abnormal*. This and this alone is *normal* Christianity.

CHAPTER IV

THE CARNAL NATURE
AND ITS CRUCIFIXION

No one can study the full-orbed truth of holiness and its synonyms without coming to grips with an important strand of Biblical teaching: the nature of the inner sin from which entire sanctification provides its complete cleansing. Implied in all that has been said about a pure heart, the baptism with the Spirit, and sanctification as cleansing is the lurking shadow of a deep stain of sin.[1]

Christian thought through the ages has been quite consistent in its view of the duality of sin. The Bible makes it very clear that sin consists both in the disobedient and rebellious deeds people do and in the dispositions, propensities, and attitudes which are part of their very natures. In the line of the gospel song, man finds himself "a sinner by choice, and an alien by birth."

It is fairly obvious that the deeds or acts which people do contrary to God's known will can be dealt with only by forgiveness and remission. On the other hand, the problem of sinful human nature can be met only through the inner changes made by the Holy Spirit which we describe as regeneration and sanctification. That there is such a problem remaining after regeneration is the virtually unanimous testimony of Christian thinkers through the ages, as well as the experience of converted people and the witness of the Word of God.

It is our task now to consider this problem of the stain of sin in the regenerate, and to examine the Biblical method of dealing with it. That such a task is extremely difficult will be denied only by those who have never undertaken it. As Dr. Howard V. Miller has so well said:

> It is extremely difficult, if not humanly impossible, to define carnality with satisfying accuracy. For here we are dealing with the most subtle and mysterious part of man's moral make-up. Indeed it would be presumptuous even to attempt to speak with sufficient clarity that all might understand our meaning concerning this matter which for centuries has been the controversial field of theological investigation. But we do believe that there are some simple cautions we may cite that will help the reader to understand the viewpoint of the writer.[2]

A. SIN AS DYNAMIC

Dr. Miller goes on to warn against thinking of sin as a substance, with some sort of tangibility or "thingness" about it. This is one of our most difficult problems. We shall later be dealing with some of the Biblical metaphors used to describe the nature of sin. Such imagery is a necessary accommodation to our sense-bound minds. We are limited by age-old habits of "thing thinking." Hence we unreflectively engage in what the philosophers call the reification of abstract qualities. We consider all reality to consist of "things." Whatever we cannot weigh, measure, count, locate in space, or picture in imagination, we tend to set aside as being unreal.

If we are ever to understand sin and salvation we must to some degree break these venerable habits of thought. We must think in dynamic rather than substantive terms. The dreadful reality of sin and the glorious reality of salvation consist, not of substances, but of relations. In technical terms, there are attributive realities which have no existence save in relation to persons, the divine and the human.

This may not be too difficult to grasp if we ask ourselves what sin would be apart from a holy God to sin against, or persons to choose the sinful acts or ways. If there were no persons in the universe, there would be no moral qualities of any sort, either good or evil. In the spiritual realm, the only substantive realities are persons. All other reality consists in what persons are and what they do.

Although it is another matter aside from our subject here, it is instructive to reflect that salvation, as well as sin, is personal and relational. It is the mending of a breach existing between persons, and the establishing of a new relationship of reconciliation and communion. Most of the difficulties arising from hard, mechanical interpretations of justification and entire sanctification could be avoided if we would train ourselves to think in dynamic and relational terms, and get above the materialistic modes of thing-thinking which come so naturally to our limited spiritual understandings.

The sin nature we are considering in this chapter, then, is not a substance—a sort of cancer to be cut out, a rotten tooth to be pulled, or a stump to be blasted out. It is rather what we *are*. It is to be located in the dynamics of personality, in the motivations, dispositions, tendencies, and attitudes of living persons. It may be conceived, but not imagined. We may think about it, but cannot picture it. It is in this light that we must turn to the teachings of the Bible.

B. The Old Testament View

The Old Testament, as well as the New, recognizes that man is not only a sinner by choice, but is sinful by nature. A. B. Davidson writes:

The Old Testament teaching regarding sin does not differ from that of the New Testament. It teaches, first, that all individual men are sinners. Second, the sinfulness of each individual is not an isolated thing, but is an instance of the general fact that mankind is sinful. And, thirdly, the sin of man can be taken away only by the forgiveness of Jehovah: "Who is a God like unto Thee, pardoning iniquity?" (Mic. vii.18).[3]

In the Old Testament, sinning is essentially rebelling against the covenant God of Israel, and results in separation from Him. "But your iniquities have separated between you and your God, and your sins have hid his face from you, that he will not hear" (Isa. 59:2). As in the New Testament, the root of sin is really the unbelief "which sees in the gift of God's love an unfriendly limitation."[4] As G. Ernest Wright has expressed it: "Sin is the violation of covenant and rebellion against God's personal lordship. It is more than an aberration or a failure which added knowledge can correct. It is a violation of relationship, a betrayal of trust."[5]

With regard to the sinfulness of human nature, the Old Testament makes two things clear. First, man as created was sinless. He became sinful by a wrong choice. Second, sin does not inhere in the physical flesh, or body. After summarizing the teaching of the Old Testament at the point of man's sinfulness, A. B. Davidson says:

The further conclusion to which the passages of the Old Testament lead us are these: first, that what is specifically called *original sin* is taught there very distinctly, i.e. "that corruption of man's whole nature which is commonly called original sin," and that it is also taught that this sin is inherited; second, that no explanation is given in the Old Testament of the rationale of this inherited corruption beyond the assumption that the race is a unity, and each member of the race is sinful because the race is sinful. In other words, in conformity with the Old Testament point of view the individual man is less referred to than the race.[6]

In Psalms 51, the Old Testament reaches the apex of its teaching on this subject. Here both transgressions (plural) and iniquity and sin (singular) are confessed. In regard to the former, the Psalmist says, "Have mercy upon me, O God, according to thy lovingkindness: according unto the multitude of thy tender mercies blot out my transgressions. For I acknowledge my transgressions: and my sin is ever before me" (vv. 1, 3). Concerning the latter, he prays, "Wash me throughly from mine iniquity, and cleanse me from my sin. Behold, I was shapen in iniquity, and in sin did my mother conceive me" (vv. 2, 5).

In the term used here for iniquity (*avon*), Schultz sees sin as a condition, a state contrary to the divine harmony.[7] Davidson says of this verse, "This sin is inherited; not he alone, but all about him are sinful. The Psalmist does not plead this as an extenuation of his act, but rather as an aggravation of his condition . . . In opposition to this condition of his he places what he knows to be the moral desire of God: 'Thou desirest truth in the inward parts: in the hidden part make me to know wisdom.' "[8]

C. The New Testament Teaching

In the New Testament, Paul deals most extensively with sin and its cure. He leaves no doubt in anyone's mind about the sinfulness of human nature apart from God. In a long passage, Rom. 3:9-18, he summarizes the Old Testament teaching on the subject. In Romans 5, he says, "Through one man sin entered into the world, and death through sin; and so death passed unto all men, for that all sinned. For as through the one man's disobedience the many were made sinners, even so through the obedience of the one shall the many be made righteous" (vv. 12, 19, A.R.V.). The same truth is expressed in Eph. 2:3: "Among whom we also all once lived in the lusts of our flesh, doing the desires of the flesh and of the mind, and were by nature children of wrath, even as the rest" (A.R.V.).

Before turning to some of Paul's vividly descriptive terms for this sinfulness of the nature of the unsanctified, let us observe five facts about sin as state or condition which are indicated in the Bible:

First, sin as state or condition is inherited in the sense that it is native to the moral dispositions of the natural man—that is, man as he is deprived of the initial moral image of God and consequently depraved in nature.

Second, this condition of sin is a tendency or disposition which is real as potential sin even when it is not expressed in actual transgressions.

Third, this sinful state is involuntary in the sense that it results from no choice of the individual.

Fourth, original sin is a consequence of, but not a penalty for, the sin of Adam and Eve.

Fifth, although altered and subdued by saving grace, the sinful condition of man's nature continues in the regenerate state until dealt with in entire sanctification.

Speaking of the view that sin consists only of what men do, James S. Stewart writes:

Certainly Paul's view went far beyond any such definition. Sin was not something a man *did:* it was something that took possession of him, something the man was, something that turned him into an open enemy of the God who loved him. It brought outward penalties: "whatsoever a man soweth, that shall he also reap" (Gal. 6:7). But far more appalling than these were its inward r e s u l t s. It tormented the conscience: "O wretched man that I am!" (Rom. 7:24). It brought the will into abject slavery: "the good that I would, I do not, but the evil which I would not, that I do" (Rom. 7:19). It destroyed fellowship with God: men were "alienated" (Col. 1:21), "without God in the world" (Eph. 2:12). It hardened the heart, and blinded the judgment, and warped the moral sense: "God gave them over to a reprobate mind" (Rom. 1:28). It destroyed life itself: "the wages of sin is death" (Rom. 6:23).[9]

D. NEW TESTAMENT DESCRIPTIONS OF INNER SIN

A full study of the New Testament teaching concerning inner sin would demand a volume in itself. We shall therefore give major attention to those aspects of the doctrine which have bearing on holiness. Even within these limitations, we must forego a complete study and content ourselves with a few of the most representative points.

The New Testament in general, and Paul in particular, use a number of different terms to describe the sinful condition or nature of man. It is spoken of as "the sin" (Rom. 6:1-2, 11, 22; 7:8, 11, 14, *passim*);[10] "the flesh" but not the physical body (Gal. 5:19, 24); "the carnal mind" or "the mind of the flesh" (Rom. 8:6-7); "carnal" (Rom. 7:14; I Cor. 3:1, 3-4), from which we get the noun we use, "carnality"; "the body of this death" (Rom. 7:24); sometimes "the old man" (Rom. 6:6; Eph. 4:22); "the body of sin" (Rom. 6:6); "the law of sin" (Rom. 7:23, 25); "the law of sin and death" (Rom. 8:2); and "the root of bitterness" (Heb. 12:15).

From this list of ten terms we can consider but three, and these because they are subject to most misunderstanding.

The first term is the flesh (*sarx*), one of the most flexible terms in the New Testament doctrine of man. It may stand for the purely human and physical, without any sense of moral disvalue, as when it is said that Christ was "born of the seed of David according to the flesh" (Rom. 1:3, A.R.V.). It may be used of human weakness in the face of temptation, as when we read, "The spirit truly is ready, but the flesh is weak" (Mark 14:38).

However, there is an important group of references in which "flesh" obviously has no connection with normal humanity, nor with the physical body, but refers to the source and seat of sin in man. Frederick C. Grant notes that the flesh in this sense is "the source not only of weakness but also of inherited tendencies to evil . . . the inborn tendency—the *yecer har-ra'*, as the Jewish teachers later called it (cf. Gen. 6:5)—became a settled habit, and the 'mind of the flesh' turns out to be 'at enmity with God' (Rom. 8:7)."[11]

Some sixteen times Paul contrasts flesh and the Spirit as being in moral conflict. A vivid illustration is found in Gal. 5:16-21, 24: "But I say, Walk by the Spirit, and ye shall not fulfil the lust of the flesh. For the flesh lusteth against the Spirit, and the Spirit against the flesh; for these are contrary the one to the other; that ye may not do the things that ye would. But if ye are led by the Spirit, ye are not under the law. Now the works of the flesh are manifest, which are these: fornication, uncleanness, laciviousness, idolatry, socery, enmities, strife, jealousies, wraths, factions, divisions, parties [heresies, marg.], envyings, drunkenness, revellings, and such like; of which I forewarn you, even as I did forewarn you, that they who practice such things shall not inherit the kingdom of God. And they that are of Christ Jesus have crucified the flesh with the passions and the lusts thereof" (A.R.V.).

In this passage "flesh" is plainly used to describe the sinful condition of the human soul. While some five of its "works" have a basis in physical impulses, the balance are sins of the spirit and mind rather than of the body. Furthermore, the physical body is not crucified, but the fleshly nature may be.

The second term we shall consider is the adjective "carnal," which is derived from *sarx* (*sarkikos*). With relation to its use in Rom. 7:14; I Cor. 3:1, 3-4; and II Cor. 1:12, W. E. Vine writes: "Speaking broadly, the carnal denotes the sinful element in man's nature, by reason of descent from Adam; the spiritual is that which comes by the regenerating [and we would add, sanctifying] operation of the Holy Spirit."[12]

In I Cor. 3:1-4, Paul summarizes the marks of the carnal Christian as envying, strife, and divisions. He contrasts the carnal person with both the natural man (2:14), that is, the unconverted person; and with the spiritual man whose character is spelled out in the list of the fruit of the Spirit in Gal. 5:22-23: "love, joy, peace, longsuffering, gentleness, goodness, faith, meekness, temperance."

E. THE CARNAL AND THE HUMAN

The King James Version uses the adjective "carnal" as the translation for "of the flesh" in Rom. 8:6-7: "For to be carnally minded is death; but to be spiritually minded is life and peace. Because the carnal mind is enmity against God: for it is not subject to the law of God, neither indeed can be." Here the apostle gives us the chief criterion of the carnal; it is that in human life which is not subject to the law of God, neither indeed can be.

One of the perplexing problems in Christian life is to distinguish between the carnal and the human. Human nature is the source of many impulses, desires, drives, tendencies, urges, weaknesses, and frailties which are not in and of themselves sinful, but which may, under the wrong circumstances, lead to sin. The carnal in man is the twisting of natural propensities, needs, and potentialities in an egocentric and sinful direction. In Dr. L. T. Corlett's well-turned phrase: "Carnality has no capital of its own." It is a perversion or corruption of the nature (Eph. 4:22). It thus takes and misdirects the use of natural and legitimate aspects of human nature.

Whether a given impulse is carnal or human may be tested by Paul's touchstone: If it has an expression in human life which is in harmony with the law and will of

God, then it is human. If it has no such proper place in a life lived in harmony with God's will, then it is carnal. For example, the major instincts—self-preservation, sex, the herd, acquisitiveness, curiosity—all have expressions in harmony with God's will and law. These are part of our natural human equipment and must be disciplined and directed (I Cor. 9:27), but can never be removed by any operation of grace within our hearts.[13]

On the other hand, there is no way whereby carnal temper, envy, resentment, animosity, cynicism, harshness, or bitterness may legitimately be expressed. These are "not subject to the law of God, neither indeed can be." They are sinful in essence and nature. From them we must be delivered by sanctifying grace if we are to live truly victorious lives.

A third term for the sinful condition of the unsanctified heart is a very picturesque phrase, used only three times, "our old man" (Rom. 6:6; Eph. 4:22; and with a somewhat different emphasis, Col. 3:9).[14] The old man is said to be "corrupt according to the deceitful lusts" and the ruling influence in the unregenerate manner of life (Eph. 4:22). Paul speaks of him only to indicate what disposition is to be made of him. He has been "crucified with him [Christ]" (Rom. 6:6), and is to be "put off or away," "stripped off" as an old suit of clothes.

This brings us to another of the great New Testament synonyms for holiness, the crucifixion or death of the sinful self, and of the self in relation to sin. With regard to original sin, the usual New Testament word is cleanse. With regard to the flesh, the carnal nature, or the old man, the cure is to put it off or put it to death.[15]

We must observe first that the New Testament speaks both of the death of the carnal principle or the sinful flesh and of the believer's death to sin. Each of these two modes of speaking must be examined.

F. The Death of Inner Sin

Two references are of key importance in regard to the death *of* inner sin: Rom. 6: 6: "Knowing this, that our old man is crucified with him, that the body of sin might be destroyed, that henceforth we should not serve sin"; and Gal. 5: 24: "And they that are Christ's have crucified the flesh with the affections and lusts."

Much ado has been made over the use of the term eradication in relation to the sinful nature. In some ways it is a good term. While not a Biblical term, it has Biblical associations, for it means "to take out, root and branch" (cf. Matt. 3: 10-12; Heb. 12: 14-15). However, there is a sense in which it may be misunderstood, as indicating the kind of "thing-thinking" we spoke of earlier in this chapter. An example of this misunderstanding, amazing in a man of his undoubted scholarship, is found in a recent book by W. E. Sangster:

> Furthermore, the exponents of eradication, admitting (as they must) that some from whom they believed all sin to be eradicated had lapsed into grievous sin again, have never been able satisfactorily to explain where the sin came from that caused this second distressing fall. To say, as they do, that the person yielded to new temptation is inadequate. Sin takes hold of us because there is something in us on which it can take hold. If we are to give credence to the idea that from some natures 'the dire root' of sin has been entirely eradicated, on what did the new sin take hold?[16]

This is one of the most common misunderstandings encountered in regard to deliverance from inner sin. "If there were no sin within, how could one transgress God's law?" The answer, naturally, is, "In precisely the same way that a holy couple first sinned in the Garden of Eden." There was no sin in Adam and Eve, unless we are to assume that God created sinful beings. James explains it thoroughly: "Each person is tempted when he is lured and enticed by his own desire. Then desire when it has conceived gives birth to sin; and sin when it is full-grown brings forth death" (Jas. 1:14-15, R.S.V.). The desire need not be sinful in order to give birth to sin. It may be perfectly legitimate, as were the desires of Adam and Eve and the desires of Jesus in the wilderness (Matt. 4:1-11; Luke 4:1-13).

However, even stronger than "eradication" are the Biblical terms "crucifixion" and "destruction." Crucifixion was sometimes swift, when the heart gave way under the shock of its brutality. It was sometimes slow, as when the victim lingered for three or four days in agony. It was always certain. It always brought an end to life. It could never refer to a gradual sanctification which fails to destroy utterly the enemy within.

G. DEATH TO SIN

The other mode of speaking of death in relation to inner sin is the believer's death *to* sin. Again we turn to Romans and Galatians for illustrative verses: "How shall we, that are dead to sin, live any longer therein? . . . he that is dead is freed from sin. Likewise reckon ye also yourselves to be dead indeed unto sin, but alive unto God through Jesus Christ our Lord" (Rom. 6:2, 7, 11); and the great confession: "I am crucified with Christ: nevertheless I live; yet not I, but Christ liveth in me: and the life which I now live in the flesh I live by the faith of the Son of God, who loved me, and gave himself for me" (Gal. 2:20).

It is obviously not the psychological self that dies in answer to the prayer:

> Let Self be crucified and slain
> > And buried deep, and all in vain
> May efforts be to rise again
> > Unless to live for OTHERS.

Dr. J. B. Chapman records an important caution at this point:

There has been, on the part of some, an effort to identify the word and idea of *self* with the flesh or carnal mind. But such a tendency is evidence of unsound philosophy and a careless use of terms. Sound holiness teachers have never used the word self in this sense. Self means "one's own individual identity," "one's own person," "personality," "individuality," "personal identity," and any claim that this is to be eradicated is of course pure nonsense. John says: "Every one that hath this hope in him purifieth himself, even as he is pure." This indicates that it is an abnormal condition from which self needs to be purified, and then that self shall be pure as Jesus is pure.[17]

Paul uses *death* in Rom. 7: 1-6, as well as elsewhere, in such a way as to show us what he means by the expression "dead to" sin. Death means separation, the breaking of all old connections, the absolving of obligations and responsibilities, freeing from former bonds.

To be "dead indeed unto sin," then, means to be freed from its presence and power, to be out from under its law and dominion. The analogy in this passage in Romans is that of a wife, bound by the law of her husband as long as he lives. When the husband dies, the wife also dies as a wife, although she lives on as a widow. But dead to the law of the married state, she is free to wed another. The application is not difficult to see. The carnal mind (the first husband) dies, and the believer (the wife) also dies to the law of the married state, and is free to be married to Another (the Lord Jesus Christ).

George Muller, the man of great faith, says little about his own personal experience with God in his *Autobiography*. But there is a record that once, urged to tell the "secret" of his spiritual successes he said:

"There was a day when I died; utterly died," and, as he spoke, he bent lower until he almost touched the floor. Continuing, he added: "Died to George Muller, his opinions, preferences, tastes and will; died to the world, its approval or censure; died to the approval or blame even of my brethren and friends and, since then, I have studied only to show myself approved unto God."[18]

It is to be noted, from Rom. 6:1-14, that baptism is both the symbol and the pledge of this death and of the life which follows. Baptism, which always comes after conversion in the New Testament, not only testifies to the washing away of the sins of the flesh, but commits the believer to an actual spiritual death with Christ and to the destruction of the body of sin: "Know ye not, that so many of us as were baptized into Jesus Christ were baptized into his death? Therefore we are buried with him by baptism into death: that like as Christ was raised up from the dead by the glory of the Father, even so we also should walk in newness of life" (vv. 3-4).

H. THE PARADOX OF DEATH AND LIFE

Herein is one of the most glorious paradoxes of Christian experience: the way to true life is death with Christ. The "baptism wherewith he was baptized" was expressed in the consecration of Gethsemane, the agonies of the Cross, and the glorious resurrection of the Easter morn. "If any man will come after me," Jesus had said to those who were already His disciples, "let him deny himself, and take up his cross, and follow me" (Matt. 16:24).

That cross is not the petty annoyances of the human life, the little sacrifices we may be called upon to make as Christians. That cross is the instrument of death. We must follow Christ into the consecration of Gethsemane, expressed in the words, "Not my will, but thine, be done" (Luke 22:42). We must follow Him on to the crucifixion of our old man, and to sin. Only then can we experience the newness of the sanctified life. Risen with Christ, we may then seek those things which are above (Col. 3:1).

CHAPTER V

THIS MATTER
OF PERFECTION

One of humanity's curious contradictions is the almost fanatical search for perfection in every realm other than the religious; and the equally fanatical rejection of the only kind of perfection open to frail mortals, the perfection of love.

It is assumed that any confession of Christian perfection leads to pride. Periodically, religious teachers arise to claim that sin in human life makes for humility. Exactly the contrary is true, for there is no greater pride than the arrogant self-sufficiency which expresses itself in sin.

As a result of these mistaken views we have the bogus humility of some "saints," exulting in the pride of sinfulness, a sort of inverted hypocrisy. E 1aB. Cherbonnier describes a cartoon in which two convicts are seen whispering about a third. One of the two says to his companion, "What I can't stand about him is his 'guiltier than thou' complex!"[1] It has been said of a modern theological movement that it just reverses the Pauline dictum and states: "Where grace abounded, sin doth

much more abound."[2] When this happens we are apt to
have what Peter Forsyth called "the phariseeism of the
publican."[3]

A. PERFECTION IN THE OLD TESTAMENT

Yet it must be admitted that both Old and New
Testaments hold forth an ideal of perfection for man in
relation to God.

In the Old Testament there are two major terms
translated "perfect." The first of these is *shalem* and its
derivatives, to which Harkavy assigns the meanings
"whole, entire, perfect . . . healthy, full of strength . . .
peace, prosperity."[4] It is a word which might be used of
a perfect weight, as in Deut. 25:15. It is used much more
often of a perfect heart, as in I Kings 8:61: "Let your
heart therefore to be perfect with the Lord our God, to
walk in his statutes, and to keep his commandments, as at
this day."

Asa (I Kings 15:14) and Hezekiah (II Kings 20:3)
are said to have had perfect hearts before the Lord. An
instructive verse is found in II Chron. 25:2, where it is
said that, for a time at least, Amaziah did what was right
in the sight of the Lord, but not with a perfect heart.
His outward conduct was irreproachable, but his heart
was not right.

The more common term for perfect in the Old Testament is *tam, tamim,* and derivatives. Harkavy expresses
the meanings of various forms of the root with such
English words as "whole, perfect and upright . . . completeness, strength, health . . . integrity . . . finished . . .
blameless."[5]

It is interesting to note that while *shalem* is never
applied to God, *tam* and *tamim* are used to describe His
way (Ps. 18:30), His law (Ps. 19:7), and His work
(Deut. 32:4). *Tam* is not used of the heart but of the
total character and conduct of the life. For example,
Noah (Gen. 6:9) and Job (1:1, 8, *passim*) are said to

have been perfect men; and Abraham is commended by God "Walk before me, and be thou perfect" (Gen. 17:1). This command is generalized in Deut. 18:13, "Thou shalt be perfect with the Lord thy God." The "blameless" of the R.S.V. in this and other Old Testament verses is totally inadequate to express the full meaning of the original.

Harold W. Perkins, in one of the classic studies of Christian perfection, writes concerning perfection in the Old Testament:

> The great advance made by Hebrew and Jewish thought was in the knowledge of the perfection of God. It is impossible to overrate the importance of this for our subject. *We are discussing, it cannot be too emphatically said, not the production of a perfect man, but union with the perfection of God.* The strong ethical bent of the prophets made them insist on holiness and righteousness as the marks of His Perfection . . . The perfection towards which man ought to strive was regarded as derivative. It came from walking with God, and could only be retained by a ceaseless communication of His Spirit. It was ethical rather than ceremonial, and in the highest and best, in Deuteronomy and Leviticus and the Testaments, it attained to the expression of love towards God and man, on which Jesus has set His seal.[6]

George Allen Turner, in his Harvard Ph.D. dissertation, points out that *tam* and *tamim* are used a total of forty-four times in the Old Testament as describing the character of the man of God. The Book of Job, Dr. Turner comments, is actually a treatise on perfection. Turner's itemized conclusions are instructive:

1. The exhortation to moral integrity, wholeness, soundness, sincerity, or perfection is very prominent in the Old Testament, especially in the prophetic literature.
2. Of the some two hundred and thirty occurrences of synonyms for perfection, about seventy-two refer to man's character.
3. A "perfect" man is one characterized by moral integrity, sincerity, and loyalty to Jehovah.

4. Such a perfection is commanded and expected of all the people of God.
5. This concept of perfection emphasizes the possibility of man's becoming like Jehovah in character.
6. Such a divine-human fellowship is based on the ideas of holiness, such as separation unto God and cleansing from all defilement whether ceremonial or moral.[7]

B. Perfection in the New Testament

The New Testament, also, has two important terms translated perfect or perfection in the English versions. One of these is *artios* with its derivatives and compounds. Its use is not as frequent as the term to which we shall turn in a moment. It carries the thought of preparedness, of full equipment, of being put to rights, or fitted to fulfill its function.[8]

Like *shalem* in the Old Testament, the forms of *artios* are never applied directly to God or Christ. Examples of its use are to be found in Luke 6:40, "The disciple is not above his master: but every one that is perfect shall be as his master"; in I Thess. 3:10, "Night and day praying exceedingly that we might see your face, and might perfect that which is lacking in your faith"; and Heb. 13:20-21, "Now the God of peace, that brought again from the dead our Lord Jesus, that great shepherd of the sheep, through the blood of the everlasting covenant, make you perfect in every good work to do his will."

The more important New Testament term for perfect and perfection is *teleios* in its various grammatical forms. There are cases in which this term is set in contrast to childhood (I Cor. 14:20 and Eph. 4:13-14), where "full grown" or "mature" is a justifiable translation. However, the New Testament use is far better expressed as "complete, conveying the idea of goodness without necessary reference to maturity."[9] Hermann Cremer states that it is, "generally, what is highest and pre-eminent . . . In a moral sense, perfected, complete, blameless."[10] In understanding its meaning, we must bear in mind the root from which it comes, *telos,* which has to do with the end or purpose inherent in the very nature of that to which it refers.

Teleios is used of the will of God (Rom. 12:2), of the heavenly tabernacle (Heb. 9:11), of the law of liberty (Jas. 1:25), of the atoning work of Christ (Luke 13:32); of both God (Matt. 5:48) and His love (I John 4:12); and of Christ (Heb. 4:9, *passim*). It is used to express God's purpose for His people in a number of important New Testament references, a few of which are:

Matt. 5:48—"Be ye therefore perfect, even as your Father which is in heaven is perfect."
I Cor. 2:6—"Howbeit we speak wisdom among them that are perfect: yet not the wisdom of this world, nor of the princes of this world, that come to nought."
John 17:23—"That they may be perfect in one; and that the world may know that thou hast sent me" (one of the concomitants of the sanctification of the disciples for which Jesus prays in verse 17).
Col. 1:28—"Warning every man, and teaching every man in all wisdom; that we may present every man perfect in Christ Jesus."
Heb. 6:1—"Therefore leaving the principles of the doctrine of Christ, let us go on unto perfection; not laying again the foundation of repentance from dead works, and of faith toward God."
Heb. 10:14—"For by one offering he hath perfected for ever them that are sanctified." Here, as in John 17:17, 23, perfection and sanctification are conjoined.

John relates *teleios* directly to love, an idea to which we shall later return: "But whoso keepeth his word, in him verily is the love of God perfected: hereby know we that we are in him" (I John 2:5); "Herein is our love made perfect, that we may have boldness in the day of judgment: because as he is, so are we in this world. There is no fear in love; but perfect love casteth out fear: because fear hath torment. He that feareth is not made perfect in love" (I John 4:17-18).

An important summary of the Biblical meaning of perfection is found in the article contributed to *A Theological Wordbook of the Bible* by R. Gregor Smith:

> To be perfect means, therefore, to be whole or sound or true; and to be perfect as the heavenly Father is perfect (Matt. 5:48, the main NT reference) means to be wholly turned, with the whole will and being, to God, as he is turned to us. This is a response of obedience and of effort carried out *in faith*. It is the call to purify our heart and to will one thing. The command falls within a religious situation, not simply a moral situation of improving our conduct by even more strenuous efforts or the like.
>
> 'Perfect' in the Bible, then, does not have a legalistic background. Nor does it have a pietist authority as though perfection could be achieved by some kind of technique of 'imitation' of Jesus. Nor do we find in the Bible any authority for speaking of perfection as the end-state of an ever-increasing goodness spreading through the individual or society. 'Be perfect' is the command of God, springing from his own life, which can strike from our hearts only one response, that of faith. Our obedience in faith is not the beginning of some vague progress on a shadowy moral way, but is the acceptance of grace, which is always whole, complete, perfect; and in the strength of this encounter our life is lived. 'Perfect' is something belonging to God and coming to us by our contact with God, not as a possession but as a gift. All that God has, and is, is perfect: it is never partial or unfulfilled. Our relation to him determines our share in this kind of wholeness.[11]

C. WHAT KIND OF PERFECTION?

But we must come to grips at once with a chief area of misunderstanding concerning the perfection to which the Bible calls and commands the people of God. It concerns the man of straw which some opponents of holiness erect and gleefully demolish. It is based, by and large, on a passage from the pen of St. Paul: "That I may know him, and the power of his resurrection, and the fellowship of his sufferings, being made conformable unto his death; if by any means I might attain unto the resurrection of the dead. Not as though I had already attained, either were already perfect: but I follow after, if that I may apprehend that for which also I am apprehended of Christ Jesus. Brethren, I count not myself to have apprehended: but this one thing I do, forgetting those things which are behind, and reaching forth unto those things which are before, I press toward the mark for the prize of the high calling of God in Christ Jesus. Let us therefore, as many as be perfect, be thus minded: and if in any thing ye be otherwise minded, God shall reveal even this unto you" (Phil. 3: 10-15).[12]

It is a sad testimony to the Biblical illiteracy of our day that any should pick out Paul's phrase, "Not as though I had already attained, either were already perfect," and use it as a scarecrow to drive men away from Christian perfection. Language could hardly make it more clear that the perfection disclaimed here is the perfection of the resurrection.

No sober or sane individual has ever claimed the perfection of the resurrection, of Adam, or such a perfection as would exclude the possibility of weakness, infirmity, mistakes in judgment, or even deformities of conduct by reason of lack of light and perfect knowledge. Biblical perfection is not the perfection of angels, but of human beings with all the limitations inherent in the species.

D. "SINLESS PERFECTION"

One special whipping boy has been the phrase "sinless perfection." Few, if any, advocates of scriptural holiness use the term, but it is commonly used by opponents of the doctrine. It would be an innocent term if all could agree that what is meant by it is that the sanctified individual does not willfully and knowingly transgress the will of God. However, it is taken to mean that the perfect individual is not able to sin, and is even rendered immune to all temptation. That such a state is never reached in this life, who would want to deny?

Henry E. Brockett was asked by a Christian friend, "Is there really nothing unholy in your life, thought, word, or deed?" His answer is memorable for its balance between the forthright confession of divine cleansing and the humility which really becomes holiness:

> If I were to make the bald, unqualified statement, "There is nothing unholy in my life," etc., it would sound like pharisaical pride which is abhorrent to me. Speaking of myself, as I am a l o n e, apart altogether from divine grace, I would say, "In me (that is, in my flesh) dwelleth no good thing." *Christ is my sanctification and I have no holiness whatever apart from Him and His indwelling.* And even with His indwelling, I am not yet entirely freed from the effects of sin and the fall, being still in a fallen condition with a mortal, corruptible body that needs "keeping under," possessing very limited knowledge and with very imperfect powers of mind, judgment, etc., all through the fall. Even if I may not be conscious of sin, there may still be faults and failures in my life which the Lord may see but of which I may not be aware. From this point of view, I still fall short of the glory of God, and hence, I need continually divine mercy and grace, the intercession of Christ, the efficacy of His precious cleansing blood and I need continually to be learning more of the will of God through His Word. I am only a sinner saved by grace. For these reasons, I would not make the unqualified statement, "There is nothing unholy in my life." It would be liable to be terribly misunderstood.[13]

It cannot properly be denied that the Scriptures distinguish clearly between sin and infirmities, the latter including all human frailties, faults, shortcomings, and weaknesses which do not have their source in purpose or intent. Howard V. Miller gives us a very necessary caution at this point:

> It must be admitted frankly that the line between mere human conduct and carnal action is very finely drawn. This is by no means begging the question. On the basis

of the most discriminating scriptural definition of sin
what may constitute sin to one is not necessarily sin to
another. This discrimination is affected by motive, and
motive is affected by training and moral perception.
Natural mannerisms are repugnant in some people but
they may be nonetheless without moral meaning. Tem-
peramental peculiarities, heredity, human crudities, all
these distort the picture and often confuse us. But we
still insist that on the basis of observation and scripture
one may have a clean heart even though his conduct
may sometimes bring criticism. Merely to brush aside
the entire question with the hasty remark that no one
has ever known one who has lived a life free from sin
is extremely superficial.[14]

It is this fact which makes judgment of another liable
to gross injustice. We must always be checked by Paul's
searching question: "Who art thou that judgest another
man's servant?" (Rom. 14: 4) As an unknown poet has
written:

Judge not: the workings of his heart and of his
       brain
     Thou canst not see.
What seems to thy dim eyes a stain
     May only be
A scar, brought home from some well-won field,
Where thou wouldst only faint and yield.

E. Perfect Love

In what, then, does Christian or evangelical perfection consist? The answer has already been suggested
in the quotations given earlier from the First Epistle of
John. It is perfect love. It is not the creation of perfect
human beings, but human beings united in perfect love
to a perfect Christ. It is the conditioning of all our
human motivations by the Spirit of holiness to the degree
that we are able to love the Lord our God with all our
heart, soul, mind, and strength; and our neighbors as
ourselves (Mark 12: 29-31). "And above all these things
put on love, which is the bond of perfectness" (Col 3: 14,

A.R.V.). "But the end of the charge is love out of a pure heart and a good conscience and faith unfeigned" (I Tim. 1: 5, A.R.V.). "Seeing ye have purified your souls in obeying the truth through the Spirit unto unfeigned love of the brethren, see that ye love one another with a pure heart fervently" (I Pet. 1: 22).[15] The great reach of this emphasis is seen when we reflect that the New Testament twice affirms that "God is love" (I John 4: 8, 16).

The ethical implications of a pure and perfect yet growing love are drawn out in Paul's great "Hymn to *Agape*" in I Corinthians 13, a portion of which reads:

> Love is very patient, very kind. Love knows no jealousy; love makes no parade, gives itself no airs, is never rude, never selfish, never irritated, never resentful; love is never glad when others go wrong, love is gladdened by goodness, always slow to expose, always eager to believe the best, always hopeful, always patient (vv. 4-7, Moffatt).

John Wesley wrote in a letter to Mr. Coughlan in 1768:

> You never learnt, either from my conversation, or preaching, or writings, that "holiness consisted in a glow of joy." I constantly told you quite the contrary: I told you it was love; the love of God and our neighbour; the image of God stamped on the heart; the life of God in the soul of man; the mind that was in Christ, enabling us to walk as Christ also walked.[16]

An almost prophetic character in saying more than he really means and seeing more than he can fully express makes the writings of Peter Forsyth at once exhilarating and exasperating. He says in one great paragraph:

> If the great revelation of God is in the Cross, and the great gift of the Cross is the Holy Spirit, then the revelation is holiness, holiness working outward as love. It is not simply sacred love, as it comes for most people to mean; but it is holiness working out into love on God's side, as our faith does on our side. God's love is the outgoing of His holiness, not as exigent law, but as redeeming grace, bent or reclaiming us, all bankrupt and defiant, to His full, rich, harmonious, eternal life. The

holiness of God is His self-sufficient perfection, whose passion is to establish itself in the unholy by gracious love. Holiness is love morally perfect; love is holiness brimming and overflowing. It is in redemption. Love is perfect, not in amount but in kind, not as intense but as holy. And holiness is perfect, not as being remote, not as being merely pure, but as it asserts itself in redeeming grace. Love, as holy, must react against sin in atonement. Holiness, as grace, must establish itself by redemption in Satan's Seat.[17]

F. Values in the Concept of Perfect Love

There are three great advantages in the description of holiness as perfect love which must not be overlooked. The first is that love is not a static, unchanging entity, but a dynamic relationship which may be both pure in that it is unmarred by mere self-interest, and at the same time growing. Indeed, a perfect love must be a growing love. Perfection in love includes within itself the necessity of an ever deepening and enriching relationship. A love which does not grow is well on the way to turning into indifference or aversion.

Since God is love, love is infinite, and provides an ideal which may well keep us on the stretch for all eternity. Yet the love of the newly sanctified may be as perfect in quality as the love of unfallen angels themselves: in Vincent Taylor's terms, "As the perfection of the bud shares in the glory of the perfect flower, and just as the opening theme in a symphony participates in the beauty of the final movement."[18]

A second advantage lies in the realm of the ethics of holiness. Love is by nature exclusive (I John 2:15). It shuts out all competing interests. It eliminates alternatives, not by the power of grim law, but by the charm and winsomeness of its object. A lad, "in love with love," may date a half dozen girls until he falls in love with one certain girl. If he is really in love with one, he loses interest in all the others. He need not be lectured and scolded and warned to stay away from the other girls. His love for the one excludes interest in all others.

In a very similar fashion, perfect love for God expels and purges away every unworthy motive and emotion. What formerly gave delight suddenly loses all its attractiveness.

A final advantage of the concept of perfect love as describing holiness is the very direct connection between the atonement in Christ and sanctification which it establishes. One of the great weaknesses in most interpretations of the Cross is that they are designed to explain justification, but have only a very tenuous and external connection with sanctification; whereas the Bible makes it plain that there is a direct and immediate relationship between the death of Christ and the sanctification of believers (Eph. 5:25-27; Heb. 13:12; I John 1:7).[19]

While not saying all there is to say about the relationship between the atonement and holiness, Vincent Taylor indicates one important point:

> Our claim, then, stands, that the experience of sanctification is based upon the Atonement, and to this submission we must now add that the experience elucidates the ministry on which it depends. This is true whether we think of sanctification as ethical perfection, as the work of the Holy Spirit, as complete victory over sin, as the attainment of the vision of God, or as perfect love. Into the Christian ideal all these elements enter; but most of all its dependence upon the work of God in Christ is seen, and its illuminative power is greatest, when it is interpreted as perfect love to God and man.[20]

One last point: perfect love as experienced in entire sanctification is not, as Bishop Anders Nygren seems to say, God's love poured through the human soul as water through a pipe. It is *our* love, kindled and conditioned by the infinite love of God. "We love, because he first loved us" (I John 4:19, A.R.V.).[21] There is no higher perfection possible to man in this life, nor is there any more desirable, than perfect love to God and to man.

CHAPTER VI

FULL

SALVATION

Perhaps no single word better expresses the message and purpose of the entire Bible than the word salvation. It has become almost a truism to state that the whole Bible is the "history of salvation." Sometimes the emphasis has been more on the history than the salvation. Sometimes the idea of the salvation involved has been obscure. But there is enough truth in the description to point out the importance of the idea of salvation in Scripture in all of its many dimensions. As Dr. J. B. Chapman states: "Salvation is the great word of the gospel, being, in a sense, a summing up of all the acts and processes involved in that glorious message of good news."[1]

A. SALVATION IN THE OLD TESTAMENT

The Old Testament is a book of salvation as well as the New. It is true that salvation in the Old Testament is a very broad term. Otto J. Baab has listed the several "goals of salvation" as including political deliverance by military might, long life, prosperity, and material blessings; but above all, the personal renunciation of self-will, pride, and sin.[2]

The Hebrew term *yasha'* (to save) is used over three hundred times in the Old Testament, and the form of salvation or deliverance was suited to the particular need, whether deliverance from the pursuing armies of Egypt (Exod. 14:13), from a premature death (Ps. 91:16), or from the stain and pollution of sin (Ps. 51:10-12). As H. H. Rowley summarizes:

> God is not alone a God of compassion. He is a saving God. His salvation manifests itself in a form appropriate to the need. Here again, therefore, while the thought of God as a saving God is constant throughout the Old Testament and lives on in the New, there is really a considerable development in the thought. At the Exodus He delivered Israel from the Egyptian bondage; at the other end of the development He is seen to deliver men from the corruption of sin. For with the perception that His compassion reached down beyond man's physical estate to his spiritual condition it was seen that His salvation reached as far as His compassion. Nowhere is He a helpless God. His resources are ever equal to His purposes.[3]

All of the great redemptive terms of the Old Testament witness to this deepening concept of salvation. God's love and grace are seen in the Old Testament as well as the New. "It was not left for the New Testament to declare that God *loves sinners*. Its distinction is that it shows *how much* He loves them."[4]

There are forgiveness and ransom and redemption in the Old Testament. God is "the everlasting God of justice, creative power, and holiness *as he seeks to save men* from their sins and to help them live a new life."[5] It is unfortunate that our concepts of Old Testament piety have been colored by the legalism and externalism of the Judaism of New Testament times. It has led us to overlook the very deep and sincere devotion of the Old Testament itself. The fact that the Psalms so adequately express the highest reaches of Christian devotion is no accident, but an eloquent testimony to the spiritual stature possible in Old Testament times.

When all this has been said, we still see that there was a forward look to salvation in the Old Testament. To put it in the technical language of the scholars, salvation takes on an eschatological aspect. It relates to the "last days," and to "the day of the Lord." The later prophets stress this most diligently. God will make a new covenant with the house of Israel (Jer. 31:31-34). A new Figure begins to fill the horizons of prophetic vision. As Hermann Schultz so eloquently put it:

> Now, just as the outward forms of sacrifice begin to fade away into shadows, the age is lighted up with the pregnant thought of a nobler sacrifice about to come. The Servant of God who represents Israel's calling, and who, uniting the sinful people with its God, becomes Himself an atonement for Israel, suffers and dies in His vocation in order to secure this reconciliation. His death, freely endured for the people, is a means of reconciliation of a new kind, an offering for sin unlike the victims slain of old. Thus, as the shadows disappear, prophecy grasps the substance.[6]

It is in the Messianic hope of the Old Testament that its doctrine of salvation reaches full flower:

> *Strengthen the weak hands,*
> *and make firm the feeble knees.*
> *Say to those who are of a fearful heart,*
> *"Be strong, fear not!*
> *Behold, your God*
> *will come with vengeance,*
> *with the recompense of God.*
> *He will come and save you."*
>
> *Then the eyes of the blind shall be opened,*
> *and the ears of the deaf unstopped;*
> *then shall the lame man leap like a hart,*
> *and the tongue of the dumb sing for joy.*

For waters shall break forth in the wilderness,
and streams in the desert;
the burning sand shall become a pool,
and the thirsty ground springs of water;
the haunt of jackals shall become a swamp,
the grass shall become reeds and rushes.

And a highway shall be there,
and it shall be called the Holy Way;
the unclean shall not pass over it,
and fools shall not err therein.
No lion shall be there,
nor shall any ravenous beast come up on it;
they shall not be found there,
but the redeemed shall walk there.
And the ransomed of the Lord shall return,
and come to Zion with singing,
with everlasting joy upon their heads;
they shall obtain joy and gladness,
and sorrow and sighing shall flee away.

(Isa. 35:3-10, R.S.V.)

It is well known that the Messianic vision took two forms in the Old Testament. It took the form of the Son of David, the victorious King; and it took the form of the Suffering Servant of Isaiah 53. It is humanly understandable that the chosen people should cherish the kingly concept and forget the suffering Redeemer. When crown and cross are both placed before us, we grasp the crown and ignore the cross. But "the shadow of the Cross falls over the Old Testament as well as the New: that is what guarantees its authenticity."[7] John Bright's searching words have a message for us today:

As for the cross of the Servant, it is not strange to us. We own to a crucified Saviour. In that we stand with the mainstream of Christian faith from the beginning onward, and we do well to do so. We enthrone that crucified Saviour in stained glass, wood, and stone—and in doctrine. To that cross we look for salvation. But we want that cross not at all. Indeed we would have it the chief business of religion to keep crosses far away. We want a Christ who suffers that we may not have to, a

Christ who lays himself down that our comfort may be undisturbed. The call to lose life that it may be found again, to take up the cross and follow, remains mysterious and offensive to us. To be sure, we labor to bring men to Christ, and we pray, "Thy kingdom come." But our labor we see as a labor of conquest and growth, successful programs and dollars. Can it be that we are seeking to build the Kingdom of the Servant—without following the Servant? If we do so, we will doubtless build a great church—but will it have anything to do with the Kingdom of God?[8]

B. Salvation in the New Testament

The Bible doctrine of salvation reaches its full expression in the New Testament, in the constant use of the verb to save, and the noun salvation. Out of a total of 150 occurrences, the verb form is used over 100 times. The term itself is as broad as the human need to which it relates. It takes in the total person, body as well as soul, so that Frederick C. Grant is fully justified in defining salvation as "the whole state of welfare or well-being of the people in right r e l a t i o n s to God."[9] Particularly in the Synoptics, "save" is frequently used in relation to physical healing (Mark 5:34; 10:52; Luke 17:19; Matt. 8:34; 14:30). Of note also is the close connection between faith for healing and for the forgiveness of sins (Mark 2:5-11).

It is of course particularly with salvation from sin that we are concerned here. W. E. Vine gives as one of the meanings of *soteria* (salvation) in the New Testament: "the present experience of God's power to deliver from the bondage of sin . . . this present experience on the part of believers is virtually equivalent to sanctification."[10] In the same vein, but working from the opposite direction, C. Ryder Smith claims: "It goes without saying that Paul's exposition of such terms as 'justify' and 'sanctify' is an exposition of salvation."[11]

C. Full Salvation

It is important to recall that salvation in the New Testament is a much broader term than conversion. Paul makes this plain in II Thess. 2:13, when he says, "But we are bound to give thanks alway to God for you, brethren beloved of the Lord, because God hath from the beginning chosen you to salvation through sanctification of the Spirit and belief of the truth." Another point closely related to this is that salvation is spoken of in all three verb tenses: we have been saved (Eph. 2:5, 8; II Tim. 1:9; Titus 3:5); we are being saved (I Cor. 1:18; II Cor. 2:15, Greek); and we shall be saved (Matt. 10:22; Acts 15:11; Rom. 13:11; I Pet. 1:5, 9).

Now it is against this background that the fathers were fully justified in distinguishing between the free salvation in justification, the full salvation in entire sanctification, and the final salvation in glorification.[12] Salvation in the New Testament sense includes all that is necessary to redeem man from sin and to qualify him for residence in a holy heaven.

That salvation in its unqualified sense includes entire sanctification is clearly seen in two passages to which reference has already been made. The first is II Thess. 2:13-14. Here salvation is said to be "through sanctification of the Spirit," not "to" or "as a preparation for" sanctification. It is also related to the gospel call, and to the final glory of our Lord Jesus Christ.

The same truth is also seen in Titus 2:11-14: "For the grace of God that bringeth salvation hath appeared to all men, teaching us that, denying ungodliness and worldly lusts, we should live soberly, righteously, and godly in this present world; looking for that blessed hope, and the glorious appearing of the great God and our Saviour Jesus Christ; who gave himself for us, that he might redeem us from all iniquity, and purify unto himself a peculiar people, zealous of good works."

Here it is seen that the salvation which comes by the grace of God includes both redemption from all iniquity and the purification unto Christ of a people for His own, marked by their zeal for good works. That this is not something to be achieved in a future life but that full salvation is for this world is seen in the apostle's insistence that we live soberly, righteously, and godly "in this present world."

D. Saved to the Uttermost

It is the writer to the Hebrews, however, who gives the most complete summary of the fact and nature of full salvation when he states: "For the law made nothing perfect, but the bringing in of a better hope did; by the which we draw nigh unto God. By so much was Jesus made a surety of a better testament. Wherefore he is able also to save them to the uttermost that come unto God by him, seeing he ever liveth to make intercession for them" (7:19, 22, 25).

It is true, much controversy has centered around the phrase "to the uttermost." Some commentators, both ancient and modern, understand this to be a purely temporal expression, "He is able to save for all time them that come." The rendering of the Revised Standard Version at this point is thoroughly objectionable: "Consequently he is able for all time to save those who draw near to God through him."

The weight of scholarly opinion, on the contrary, is that the phrase indicates degree, not duration; and that what is in view here is not the length of time for which Christ saves, but the extent of His salvation.

Henry Alford notes that some take the phrase "to the uttermost" (Greek, *eis to panteles*) to refer to time, and says, "But this is not the usage of the word. Bleek has shown by very many instances, that *completeness,* not duration, is its idea: as indeed its etymology would lead us to suspect."[13]

The Expositor's Greek Testament likewise states: "The phrase uniformly means 'completely', 'thoroughly', as in Luke xiii.11."[14] Dr. A. M. Hills also defines it as "completely, entirely, perfectly," and combines both the temporal and the qualitative ideas in a very happy phrase, "clear to the end of every possible need of the soul."[15]

Among the recent translations of the verse, none is better than J. B. Phillips' rendering, "This means that he can save fully and completely those who approach God through him."[16] *The Amplified New Testament* gives "completely, perfectly, finally and for all time and eternity" as its amplification of the phrase "to the uttermost."[17]

Dr. H. Orton Wiley, in his masterful exposition of Hebrews, states concerning this passage:

> The writer has shown that perfection does not come by the Levitical priesthood, but he does say in effect, if not in words, that perfection does come through Christ. He does not use the term perfection, *teleiosis*, but the more general term *sozein*, "to save"; to which is added the phrase *eis to panteles*, which means *"completely,"* "perfectly," and "to the uttermost," as indicated above. This is a strong expression ascribing to Christ a salvation which includes all possible perfections, all beneficent ends, pardon of sins, sanctification, our "fruit unto holiness, and the end everlasting life" (Rom. 6:22). This verse justifies the reference to Jesus as the Sanctifier as given in 2:11, and this sanctification in its wider meaning includes the cleansing from all sin and the indwelling of the Holy Spirit.[18]

In a very important application, Dr. Wiley points out the only other place in the New Testament where the Greek phrase in question is used, in Luke 13:11. Here it is spoken concerning:

> . . . the woman who was bowed together by the spirit of infirmity for eighteen years and could in no wise

lift up herself, the Greek words being identical with those above. She could not lift up herself "wholly" or "to the uttermost." As through the miraculous healing she was enabled to lift up herself to her full height physically, so the writer of this Epistle tells us that Jesus also enables men to lift themselves up to their full height spiritually. God never destroys in man any faculty which He has created, nor does He add any; but He does so cleanse from all sin and unrighteousness that a man may stretch himself up to his full height. To what heights the Spirit of holiness may raise and sustain the soul that is fully committed to Him we cannot know; but we do know that whatever heights are attained are due to the new humanity, perfected in Christ by obedience and suffering, and now imparted to His people by the power of the Holy Spirit.[19]

Thus the incomparable Christ is presented to us as the perfect Saviour, delivering not only from the penalty and power of sins committed, but from the very stain of sin itself. The Lord Jesus Christ is made unto us by God "wisdom, and righteousness, and sanctification, and redemption" (I Cor. 1:30).

Here is salvation not only set forth in its great stages, but portrayed in its completeness. Christ is made our Wisdom in the conviction of the Spirit which brings that "fear of the Lord" which is the "beginning of wisdom" (Prov. 9:10). In the repentance and faith of justification, He becomes our Righteousness (Rom. 5:17). In a second crisis of consecration (Rom. 6:13) and faith (Acts 20:32), Christ becomes our Sanctification (Acts 26:18). Along with wisdom, righteousness, and sanctification comes the present possession of an undimming hope of redemption, to include our bodies as well as our inner selves (Rom. 8:11, 23).

NOTES

NOTES FOR INTRODUCTION

1. See Arnold S. Nash, ed., *Protestant Thought in the Twentieth Century: Whence and Whither?* (New York: The Macmillan Company, 1951) for an indication of the widespread collapse of the old liberalism, and the scope of this reconstruction.

2. Article X, "The Articles of Faith," "Constitution of the Church of the Nazarene," *Manual*, 1928, 1932, 1936, 1940, 1944, 1948, 1952, 1956.

NOTES TO CHAPTER I

1. C. Ryder Smith, *The Bible Doctrine of Man* (London: The Epworth Press, 1951), pp. 39-40; and Robert Young, *Analytical Concordance to the Bible* (Grand Rapids: Wm. B. Eerdmans Publishing Company, n.d.), *in loco.*

2. Cf. H. Orton Wiley, *Christian Theology* (Kansas City, Mo.: Nazarene Publishing House, 1940), I, 370 f.; Norman H. Snaith, *The Distinctive Ideas of the Old Testament* (Philadelphia: The Westminster Press, 1946), pp. 100 ff.; Hermann Schultz, *Old Testament Theology,* trans. by J. A. Paterson (Edinburgh: T. and T. Clark, 1909), II, 167-77; A. B. Davidson, *The Theology of the Old Testament* (Edinburgh: T. and T. Clark, 1904), p. 151; and Edmond Jacob, *Theology of the Old Testament* (New York: Harper Brothers, 1958), p. 86.

3. Isa. 1:4; 5:19; 5:24; 10:17; 10:20, etc.; 40:25; 41:14, 16, 20, etc. Students of the unity of Isaiah will note that this expression occurs fourteen times in Isaiah 1—39; and sixteen times in Isaiah 40—66; and only seven other times in the entire Old Testament.

4. The Bible makes no distinction between sanctification and holiness. Both are English terms used to translate the same Hebrew and Greek words. With regard to the ceremonial and ethical meanings of holiness, cf. George Allen Turner, *The More Excellent Way* (Winona Lake The Light and Life Press, 1952), pp. 21-38, where a very similar distinction is noted in the Old Testament between the religious or Temple concept, and the prophetic or synagogue concept. The volume is a reprint of Professor Turner's Ph.D thesis at Harvard University.

5. *Positive Preaching and the Modern Mind* (New York: George H. Doran Company, 1907), p. 310. Also cf. Davidson, *op.*

cit., p. 258, Snaith, *op. cit.*, pp. 56-57; Smith, *op. cit.*, p. 50; Jacob, *op. cit.*, p. 92; Hermann Cremer, *Supplement to the Biblico-Theological Lexicon of New Testament Greek* (Edinburgh: T. and T. Clark, 1886), p. 596, "What is holy is pure, and demands purity . . . There is no holiness without purity," and pp. 596-601, where it is argued that separation TO God implies separation FROM sin.

6. Among the lexicons, Liddell and Scott, 1854; Hermann Cremer, 1880; Edward Robinson, 1883; J. H. Thayer, 1889; Westcott and Hort (supplement to *The New Testament in the Original Greek*), 1889; G. Abbott-Smith, 1948; Arndt and Gingrich, 1957 ("make holy" as the second meaning). Among the dictionaries, *The Oxford English Dictionary*, Vol. IX, 1933; *The New Century Dictionary*, 1944; *The American College Dictionary*, 1953; and *Webster's New International Dictionary*, 1959.

7. E.g., by W. E. Sangster, *The Pure in Heart* (New York: Abingdon Press, 1954), p. 28.

8. *The Greek Testament* (Chicago: The Moody Press, reprint 1958), I, 880.

9. Cf. James S. Stewart, *A Man in Christ* (New York: Harper and Brothers, n.d.), pp. 1-15.

10. Including I and II Corinthians and Romans. Chronologies of Paul's ministry differ in detail, but A.D. 52-56 would seem a reasonable dating for the third missionary journey. Some scholars still date Galatians with this group, but there is strong internal evidence for an earlier time for Galatians, which would make it the first of Paul's letters. Cf. Francis Davidson, ed., *The New Bible Commentary* (Grand Rapids: Wm. B. Eerdmans Co., 1956), pp. 69-70, 919, 1001-2.

11. The best Greek texts use *hagiotes* here, and this is followed by the American Standard and Revised Standard Versions. The King James Version, following the received text of 1611, transaltes: "For our rejoicing is this, the testimony of our conscience, that in simplicity and godly sincerity, not with fleshly wisdom, but by the grace of God, we have had our conversation in the world, and more abundantly to you-ward."

12. Rom. 5:12-21 actually provides a transition from the discussion of justification (how a righteous God can pardon the sins of men) to the discussion of sanctification (how a holy God deals with the sinfulness of human nature).

13. Grand Rapids: Zondervan Publishing House, 1958.

14. Herbert A. Youtz in *A Dictionary of Religion and Ethics*, edited by Shailer Mathews and G. B. Smith (New York: The Macmillan Company, 1921), p. 397.

15. R. H. Coats in *The Encyclopedia of Religion and Ethics*, James Hastings, ed. (New York: Charles Scribner's Sons, 1924), XI, 181.

16. Harris F. Rall in *The International Standard Bible Encyclopedia*, James Orr, ed. (Grand Rapids: Wm. B. Eerdmans Co., 1943), IV, 2682.

17. H. T. Cremer in *The New Schaff-Herzog Encyclopedia of*

Religious Knowledge (Grand Rapids: Baker Book House, 1950), X, 199.

18. *Lutheran Cyclopedia*, E. L. Lueker, ed. (St. Louis, Mo.; Concordia Publishing House, 1954), p. 942.

19. Kenneth J. Foreman in *The Twentieth Century Encyclopedia of Religious Knowledge*, L. A. Loetscher, ed. in chief (Grand Rapids: Baker Book House, 1955), p. 1053.

20. Charles A. Trentham, *Encyclopedia of Southern Baptists* (Nashville, Tenn.: Broadman Press, 1958), p. 1184.

21. *Systematic Theology* (New York: Charles Scribner and Co., 1872), III, 213.

22. *Ibid.*, p. 221.

23. *Op. cit.*, pp. 152-53.

24. The author has discussed this in a former work, *Conflicting Concepts of Holiness* (Kansas City, Mo.: Beacon Hill Press, 1953), pp. 29-44, and in a co-operative volume entitled *Exploring Our Christian Faith*, Chapter XVII.

25. The Greek term for holiness here is *hosiotes*, from *hosios*—as also in Eph. 4:24; I Thess. 2:10; I Tim. 2:8; Titus 1:8. These terms are used less frequently than *hagios* and its derivatives, and more often of God or Christ than of men. Cremer defines the root as denoting primarily "whether the piety which is based upon divine as well as human right, whether the word be used to demand such a piety or is predicated of those who possess it . . . where stress is laid upon their relationship to God" (*Biblico-Theological Lexicon of New Testament Greek*, Edinburgh: T. and T. Clark, 1880, p. 462). W. E. Vine defines the noun as "that quality of holiness which is manifested in those who have regard equally to grace and truth; it involves a right relation to God"; and the adjective as "religiously right, holy, as opposed to what is unrighteous or polluted" (*Expository Dictionary of New Testament Words*, London: Oliphants Ltd., 1940, II, 226-27). The major difference between this term and the more common *hagios* derivatives is that it never means consecrated or set apart. Its meaning is always purity, holy, or holiness.

NOTES TO CHAPTER II

1. Cf. the statement: Entire sanctification "is wrought by the baptism with the Holy Spirit, and comprehends in one experience the cleansing of the heart from sin and the abiding indwelling presence of the Holy Spirit, empowering the believer for life and service" (Article X, "Articles of Faith," "Constitution of the Church of the Nazarene," *Manual*). The subject of this chapter receives one of its finest recent treatments in William Greathouse, *The Fullness of the Spirit* (Kansas City, Mo.: Beacon Hill Press, 1958), which may be commended without reservation.

2. John 14:15-17; 14:26-27; 15:26-27; 16:7-11; 16:13-15.

3. John 3:6; Mark 3:29; Luke 11:13; John 7:39; Mark 13:11.

4. The Greek *Parakletos* means literally "one called alongside to help." Jesus himself is called the *Parakletos* (translated "Advo-

cate") in I John 2:1, and this idea is suggested in our Lord's expression "another Paraclete" (John 14:16). "Comforter" is not entirely inept, if its derivation is remembered: *con*—"with"; and *fortare*—"power, might."

5. *Introducing the New Testament,* rev. ed. (Philadelphia: Westminster Press, 1957), p. 68 n.

6. Some have mistakenly applied Paul's reference to the unity of the Church in I Cor. 12:13 to the baptism *with* the Holy Spirit. A careful reading of the passage will show that what is in question is not a baptism *with* the Spirit, but a work done *by* the Spirit, initiating the believer by (water) baptism into the body of Christ. John Wesley says of this verse, *"For by that one Spirit, which we received in baptism, we were all united in one body" (Explanatory Notes on the New Testament, in loco).*

7. "Baptized with," twice; "filled with" or "full of," ten times.

8. *New Testament Holiness* (London: The Epworth Press, 1902), p. 66.

9. A. M. Hunter, *Interpreting Paul's Gospel* (Philadelphia: Westminster Press, 1954), p. 108.

10. *Veni Creator: Thoughts on the Person and Work of the Holy Spirit of Promise* (London: Hodder and Stoughton, 1895), p. 211.

11. *Ibid.,* p. 226.

12. New York: Fleming H. Revell Co., 1910. Pp. 174, 176.

13. "The Spirit in the New Testament," *The Doctrine of the Holy Spirit.* The Headingly Lectures (London: The Epworth Press, 1937), p. 50. Taylor's developed doctrine of sanctification is a modified growth theory.

14. Editorial, "What Is the Christian Answer?" *Theology Today,* Vol. III, No. 1 (April, 1946), p. 9. A portion of this same passage is quoted by James S. Stewart in *A Faith to Proclaim* (New York: Charles Scribner's Sons, 1953), pp. 144-45.

15. Anderson, Indiana: The Warner Press, 1945. Pp. 195-210.

16. Francis Davidson, ed., *The New Bible Commentary* (Grand Rapids, Michigan: Wm. B. Eerdmans Publishing Co., 1956, p. 963.

17. *Secret Power* (Chicago: The Bible Institute Colportage Association, 1908), p. 16.

18. *Ibid.,* p. 50.

NOTES TO CHAPTER III

1. Alexander Harkavy, *Student's Hebrew and Chaldee Dictionary to the Old Testament* (New York: Hebrew Publishing Co., 1914), p. 214.

2. *The Path to Perfection* (New York: Abingdon-Cokesbury Press, 1943), pp. 36-52. Sangster admittedly based his survey chiefly on *The Plain Account of Christian Perfection,* which could very well be one reason for some of his interpretations: as, for example, that Mr. Wesley taught that sin consists only in acts. Wesley's sermon "Sin in Believers" should forever dispel that illusion.

3. *The Plain Account of Christian Perfection* (Boston: The Christian Witness Co., n.d.), pp. 29-30.

4. *Expository Dictionary of New Testament Words* (London: Oliphant's Ltd., 1940), III, 231.

5. *Biblico-Theological Lexicon of New Testament Greek* (Edinburgh: T. and T. Clark, 1880), p. 315.

6. In Revelation, John uses *katharos* in a sense which may well symbolize moral and spiritual purity when he speaks of the fine linen of the saints, clean and white (19:8, 14); the pure gold of the New Jerusalem (21:18, 21); and the pure water of the river of life (22:1).

7. In a chapel address, Pasadena College, fall, 1956.

8. Cf. the statement to this effect in C. Ryder Smith, "The Coexistence of Grace and Sin," *The Bible Doctrine of Grace* (London: The Epworth Press, 1956), pp. 124-40.

9. Emil Brunner, in *The Christian Understanding of Man*, Vol. II of the Report of the Oxford Conference on Church, Community and State (London: George Allen and Unwin Ltd., 1938), p. 161.

10. *Synonyms of the Old Testament* (Grand Rapids, Michigan: Wm. B. Eerdmans Publishing Company, 1956), p. 65.

11. *The Bible Doctrine of Man* (London: The Epworth Press, 1951), p. 151.

NOTES TO CHAPTER IV

1. Cf., "We believe that entire sanctification is that act of God, subsequent to regeneration, by which believers are made free from original sin, or depravity, and brought into a state of entire devotement to God, and the holy obedience of love made perfect" (Article X, "The Articles of Faith," "Constitution of the Church of the Nazarene," *Manual*).

2. *The Sin Problem* (Kansas City, Mo.: Beacon Hill Press, 1947), p. 71.

3. *Theology of the Old Testament* (Edinburgh: T. and T. Clark, 1904), p. 217.

4. Hermann Schultz, *Old Testament Theology*. Trans. by J. A. Paterson. (Edinburgh: T. and T. Clark, 1909), II, 305.

5. G. Ernest Wright and Reginald Fuller, *The Book of the Acts of God* (New York: Doubleday and Co., 1957), p. 94.

6. *Op. cit.*, p. 225. Other Old Testament scholars are less definite, and C. Ryder Smith argues that there is no concept of original sin in the Old Testament (*The Bible Doctrine of Sin*, pp. 37 ff.). The discrepancy may well lie in the fact that Smith seeks a doctrine and finds none; Davidson surveys the evidence, and concludes that the doctrine is implied in the statements made. The logic of the case would certainly seem to rest with Dr. Davidson.

7. *Op. cit.*, p. 306.

8. *Op. cit.*, pp. 232-33.

9. *A Man in Christ* (New York: Harper and Brothers, n.d.), pp. 106-7.

10. English translations omit the definite article "the," which is present in the Greek. A. M. Hills says: "At the outset we would call attention to the striking fact, as it seems to us, that the Greek noun for sin (*hamartia*) is found thirty-six times between Rom. 5:12 and Rom. 8:10, and in twenty-nine of these times it has the definite article, 'the,' before it, and is always in the singular number. We cannot help believing that the expression, 'the sin,' 'the sin,' so often repeated, means a particular kind of sin, namely, 'indwelling sin,' 'inherited sin,' 'the sin principle,' 'depravity.' In several of the other seven times, when it has no article, it manifestly means actual sin."—*Holiness in the Book of Romans* (Kansas City, Mo.: Beacon Hill Press, 1950), p. 15. Dr. Hills quotes Whedon, Alford, Godet, and Lange in support. Sanday and Headlam, also state: "There is an under-current all through the passage, showing how there was something else at work besides the guilt of individuals. That 'something' is the effect of Adam's Fall. The Fall gave the predisposition to sin; and the Fall linked together sin and death."—*The Epistle to the Romans.* "International Critical Commentary" (New York: Charles Scribner's Sons, 1896), p. 134.

11. *An Introduction to New Testament Thought* (New York: Abingdon-Cokesbury Press, 1950), p. 168. Henry E. Brockett, following A. Paget Wilkes, would distinguish between "flesh" and "indwelling sin" in every reference (*Scriptural Freedom from Sin.* Kansas City, Mo.: Beacon Hill Press, 1941. Pp. 121-22). Admitting the wide variety of uses the New Testament makes of "flesh," it still seems clear that it is, on occasion, used as denoting the sin principle.

12. *Expository Dictionary of New Testament Words* (London: Oliphants Ltd., 1940), II, 108.

13. Cf. the chapter on "Scriptural Suppression," Miller, *op. cit.*, pp. 44-50.

14. It should be recognized that "the old man" may refer to the whole of the former sinful life as well as the cause or root from which that life comes. Cf., on this point, J. B. Chapman, *The Terminology of Holiness* (Kansas City, Mo.: Beacon Hill Press, 1947), p. 108; and Cecil Rowland Paul, "A Study of the Sixth Chapter of Romans with Special Reference to the Question of Freedom from Sin" (Unpublished B.D. thesis, Nazarene Theological Seminary, 1958).

15. A slightly different emphasis is found in Col. 2:11, where the "putting off the body of the sins of the flesh by the circumcision of Christ" in a "circumcision made without hands" (cf. Deut. 31:6) is a reference to the cleansing of the soul. Cf. John Wesley's sermon on "The Circumcision of the Heart," where it is defined as "that habitual disposition of soul which in the sacred writings is termed holiness; and which directly implies, the being cleansed from sin, 'from all filthiness both of flesh and spirit;' and, by consequence, the being endued with those virtues, which were also in Christ Jesus; the being so 'renewed in the spirit of

our mind,' as to be 'perfect as our Father in heaven is perfect'"
(*Sermons*, I, 148).

16. *The Pure in Heart:* A Study in Christian Sanctity (New
York: The Abingdon Press, 1954), p. 228.

17. *Op. cit.*, p. 72

18. Quoted by Sangster, *op. cit.*, p. 141.

NOTES TO CHAPTER V

1. *Hardness of Heart* (Garden City, N.Y.: Doubleday and
Company, Inc., 1955), p. 118. Cherbonnier gives one of the most
trenchant criticisms of the Calvinistic form of the doctrine of
original sin to appear in many a year. His analysis of existentialist and Pelagian views is no less striking.

2. Credited to Paul Scherer, with regard to the neo-orthodox
and existentialist identification of humanity and sinfulness.

3. *Positive Preaching and the Modern Mind* (New York:
George H. Doran, 1907). Forsyth falls under his own condemna-
tion in his book on *Christian Perfection,* which is neither perfection nor Christian.

4. Alexander Harkavy, *Student's Hebrew and Chaldee Dictionary to the Old Testament* (New York: Hebrew Publishing
Co., 1914), p. 727.

5. *Ibid.*, pp. 766-69.

6. *The Doctrine of Christian or Evangelical Perfection* (London: The Epworth Press, 1927), pp. 52-53. Italics in the original.

7. *The More Excellent Way:* The Scriptural Basis of the
Wesleyan Message (Winona Lake, Indiana: Light and Life Press,
1952), pp. 32-38.

8. Cf. Perkins, *op. cit.*, pp. 54-56.

9. W. E. Vine, *Expository Dictionary of New Testament Words*
(London: Oliphants Ltd., 1940), III, 174. Vine also notes the
meanings "fully grown," "mature," which may be used with
either physical or ethical import.

10. *Biblico-Theological Lexicon of New Testament Greek*
(Edinburgh: T. and T. Clark, 1880), pp. 542-45.

11. "Perfect," *A Theological Word Book of the Bible*, Alan
Richardson, ed. (London: SCM Press, Ltd., 1950), p. 167.

12. No serious student of this subject can afford to miss John
Wesley's sermons "On Christian Perfection" (Phil. 3:12), *Sermons*,
I (London edition), 355-68; and "On Perfection" (Heb. 6:1), II,
167-77. Cf. Perkins, *op. cit.*, p. 15: "This gift may be called Christian
Perfection, seeing that it is to be received by one who follows and
believes in Jesus the Christ. Or it may be spoken of as Evangelical Perfection inasmuch as it is set before us as a part, and the
crowning part, of the Evangel."

13. *Scriptural Freedom from Sin* (Kansas City, Mo.:   Beacon
Hill Press, 1941), p. 50.

14. *The Sin Problem* (Kansas City, Mo.:   Beacon Hill Press,
1947), p. 72. The especially valuable treatment of this problem
by Lewis T. Corlett, "Holiness and Human Frailties," is highly

recommended: *Holiness the Harmonizing Experience* (Kansas City, Mo.: Beacon Hill Press, 1951), pp. 61-76.

15. Some Greek texts lack the adjective "pure" as modifying "heart," and consequently it is omitted in the revised versions. The idea is contained in the verb, "ye have purified your souls."

16. Quoted by Perkins, *op. cit.*, pp. 209-10.

17. *Positive Preaching and the Modern Mind*, p. 213.

18. *Forgiveness and Reconciliation* (London: Macmillan and Co., Ltd., 1941), p. 214. Cf. also J. B. Chapman, *The Terminology of Holiness* (Kansas City, Mo.: Beacon Hill Press, 1947), p. 79: "After holiness, perfect love is perhaps the most useful of the terms by which to describe the estate of the entirely sanctified. This was a favorite term with John Wesley. His opposers compelled Wesley to come to the defense of the term perfection, but there is evidence that this was not his choice. The term perfect love is scriptural, and while involving a high profession, is also becoming in modesty; for it indicates much grace, but makes no claim to either superior light or outstanding advancement in growth and maturity."

19. Cf. the discussion in Gustaf Aulen, *Christus Victor*. Trans. by A. G. Hebert (New York: The Macmillan Co., 1931), pp. 60, 167.

20. *Op. cit.*, p. 266.

21. The best Greek texts omit "him." Of course, we love Him because He first loved us; but even more, we love at all (with *agape* love) only because He awakened that kind of love in our hearts by first loving us.

NOTES TO CHAPTER VI

1. *The Terminology of Holiness* (Kansas City, Mo.: Beacon Hill Press, 1947), p. 57.

2. *Theology of the Old Testament* (New York: Abingdon-Cokesbury Press, 1949), pp. 115-20.

3. *The Unity of the Bible* (Philadelphia: The Westminster Press, 1953), pp. 67-68.

4. C. Ryder Smith, *The Bible Doctrine of Sin* (London: The Epworth Press, 1953), p. 56.

5. Baab, *op. cit.*, p. 121.

6. *Old Testament Theology*. Trans. by J. A. Paterson (Edinburgh: T. and T. Clark, 1909), II, 96.

7. A. G. Hebert, "Le Dessein de l'Esperance messianique," *Dieu Vivant*, 1946, No. 6, p. 86: quoted by Albert Gelin, *The Key Concepts of the Old Testament* (New York: Sheed and Ward, 1955), p. 37.

8. *The Kingdom of God* (New York: The Abingdon Press, 1953), p. 154.

9. *Introduction to New Testament Thought* (New York: The Abingdon Press, 1950), p. 247.

10. *Expository Dictionary of New Testament Words* (London: Oliphants Ltd., 1940, III, 316.

11. *The Bible Doctrine of Grace* (London: The Epworth Press, 1956), p. 74.

12. The use of the expression goes back to John Wesley. Cf. J. B. Chapman, *op. cit.,* p. 64. Note also the many times in the New Testament where the term salvation is used in an absolute sense, without qualification, as in Acts 4:12; 13:26; 16:17; Rom. 1:16; 10:1, 10; II Cor. 1:6; 7:10; Eph. 1:13; Phil. 1:28; 2:12; Heb. 2:3.

13. *The Greek Testament* (Chicago: The Moody Press, reprint 1958), IV, 143.

14. W. Robertson Nicoll, ed. (Grand Rapids, Michigan: Wm. B. Eerdmans Publishing Co., reprint), IV, 316.

15. *The Uttermost Salvation* (Kansas City, Mo.:   Nazarene Publishing House, 1927), p. 7.

16. *Letters to Young Churches* (New York: The Macmillan Company, 1950) or *The New Testament in Modern English* (New York: The Macmillan Company, 1958), *in loco.*

17. Cf. also the discussion in Charles Ewing Brown, *The Meaning of Sanctification* (Anderson, Indiana: The Warner Press, 1945), pp. 192-94.

18. *The Epistle to the Hebrews* (Kansas City, Mo.: Beacon Hill Press, 1959), p. 254. The entire Book of Hebrews is an eloquent presentation of the nature and necessity of full salvation.

19. *Ibid.,* pp. 254-55.

INDEXES

INDEX OF SUBJECTS AND PROPER NAMES